Adolescents in Turmoil,
Parents Under Stress:
A Pastoral Ministry Primer

Integration Books

STUDIES IN PASTORAL PSYCHOLOGY,
THEOLOGY, AND SPIRITUALITY

Robert J. Wicks,
General Editor

also in this series

Clinical Handbook of Pastoral Counseling
R. Wicks, R. Parsons, and D. Capps (Eds.)

Adolescents in Turmoil, Parents Under Stress:

A Pastoral Ministry Primer

Richard D. Parsons

Integration Books

paulist press / new york and mahwah

Acknowledgement
The Publisher gratefully acknowledges Mills Music for the use of the lyrics for *Solitude* by Ellington, Mills, and DeLange. Copyright 1934 by Mills Music, Inc. Copyright renewed. Used with permission. All rights reserved.

Library of Congress Cataloging-in-Publication Data

Parsons, Richard D.
    Adolescents in turmoil, parents under stress.

    (Integration books)
    1. Adolescent psychology.   2. Pastoral
counseling.   3. Parent and child.   I. Title.
II. Series.
BF724.P37   1986   155.5   86-30462
ISBN 0-8091-2855-1

Published by Paulist Press
997 Macarthur Boulevard
Mahwah, New Jersey 07430

Printed and bound in the
United States of America

Contents

Throughout the pages of this text emphasis is given to the importance of providing adolescents with the *unconditional love* they deserve, the *guidance* they need and the *opportunities* they desire.

It has been my good fortune to be blessed with two parents who gave me all I could have ever asked for or needed. Their love, guidance and support has been without end and it is, therefore, with much love, that I dedicate this book to my mom and dad,

Marie and Conrad Parsons

Introduction

Anna Freud once said that when there is no turmoil in adolescence, that in itself is worthy of note. This comment should not surprise anyone who regularly interacts with adolescents. Physiological, emotional, and social changes during this period can—and often do—erupt into episodes of upheaval. Such dramatic occurrences not only are stressful for the youths themselves but are also a challenge for those who must deal interpersonally with them.

This stormy time need not be a time for despair. It is a time of confusion and pressure brought on by the chaos that often takes place when young people move toward independence through adolescent experimentation. Despite this, much is known about this period which can help both the adolescents and the adults who are involved with them. And this is in essence the goal of this book.

The author presents sound clinical information in a manner which is clear, concise and helpful. In addition his reflections naturally flow from a Christian value base which makes the material not only psychologically useful but also appropriate from an ethical standpoint.

Though brief, there is much to be learned in this volume on essential areas such as communications, adolescent independence, sexuality, drug use, loneliness and alienation, and the horrible problem of adolescent suicide. In each area, numerous illustrations and basic points enable anyone who deals with adolescents and the adults in their lives to assume a helpful role.

Probably the key to this book is its hopeful tone. Adolescence is not played down or seen through rose colored glasses but neither is it seen through the eyes of despair and helplessness. Rather it is seen as a challenge to be understood and assertively met. It is a time when all adults—even the parents, maybe *especially* the parents—

need to see themselves as "youth ministers." And given all the help this book offers along these lines, the possibility of this becoming a reality is, I believe, greatly increased.

Robert J. Wicks
Series Editor

Preface

Adolescence is a dramatic stage in human development. So, in reflecting on the topic prior to creating an outline on the subject, it was not surprising to first recall an incident that occurred several years ago. It was the end of a full day at the office and I was interrupted by a sharp, rapid series of knocks at the door. Startled and confused, I got up from behind my desk, walked over to the door and opened it to find a man, a woman, and a boy of about fifteen years of age.

> "You have to help! We heard you talk at . . . well never mind . . . we . . . we . . . Tom and I just can't take it anymore!" the mother began.

Now very confused, I gathered as much composure as possible and suggested that these "strangers" at my door enter, rather than continue the discussion in the hallway. The parents entered, all the time excusing themselves for this unorthodox, perhaps rude intrusion. After introducing themselves, and Tommy, their adolescent son, they began to explain the recent events which led them to my doorstep. Almost in unison both parents stated that an absolute crisis was gripping their family and that they were on the brink of a catastrophe. They said they believed that I was their last hope! Further discussion revealed that the conditions leading this family to my doorstep were neither of crisis proportion, nor of a catastrophic nature. Similarly our discussion revealed that I was far from the last hope! Yet, even though the events surrounding this encounter were less than catastrophic, the pain, anguish and total sense of impotence experienced by the parents, and the dread, confusion, and helplessness reflected by the adolescent, were most certainly real and quite paralyzing.

Although most introductions to my clients occur through more traditional avenues, I have long ago come to appreciate and antici-

pate the unexpected. When ministering to the adolescent and his/
her family one must be open to the "call" at any time.

Reading through the above brief scenario probably elicits one's
own special memories—e.g., memories of the family who met you
after Sunday services and whose simple "Can we talk?" opened a
floodgate of marital discord, alcoholism, major depression, and other
destructively painful human experiences; memories of answering a
telephone call or a knock at the door only to find a parent or a youth
in tears and despair; memories of the youth in a class, at a service,
or in an activity, whose very expression reflects the pain of a youth
trapped by drugs, unwanted pregnancy, family conflict, and desperation around the events of his/her life which was further exacerbated
by his/her sense of isolation and abandonment.

The fact that adolescents and their parents need support and assistance as they mature through this special period of life is clearly
evident. What may not be as evident is that the opportunity for providing such support often rests with those involved in parish and
school ministry (e.g., clergy, religious, school personnel, DRE's,
youth ministers, etc.). Further, what is often not fully appreciated is
that those with the greatest opportunity to serve may be the least
prepared to do so.

Assisting families through the adolescent period of storm and
stress requires an *understanding* of the special demands of this developmental period and *development* of the skills needed to intervene with individuals and families in need. It is in the hope of
facilitating an understanding of the adolescent turmoil and a development of the skills needed for ministering to youths and their families that this book was written.

Adolescents in Turmoil, Parents Under Stress blends theoretical
information with practical suggestions. The intent is to provide both
a broad framework from which to approach one's own specific concerns and a way to demonstrate how this knowledge can be applied
in day to day ministry. A unique focus of the book is its integration
of Christian values and beliefs with the methods of psychology. The
cognitive-behavioral psychological orientation taken throughout the
book is blended with the Christian value-based orientation to provide a useful and valid paradigm for understanding and effectively
caring for adolescents.

The first three chapters provide a foundation and framework for working with the adolescent. Chapter 1 highlights the importance of "the relationship." In line with this, Chapter 3 provides guidelines for developing the needed channels of communication between adolescents and adults. Chapter 2 presents an overview of adolescence as a developmental stage by highlighting the unique demands and needs experienced by the adolescent.

The next four chapters discuss several of the "normative" crises confronting youth, such as becoming independent (Chapter 4), sexuality (Chapter 5), the question of drugs (Chapter 6), and becoming responsible (Chapter 7). Following this, Chapter 8, "Loneliness and Alienation," and Chapter 9, "Suicide," present an overview to two of the more serious—and "dark"—experiences of adolescence.

The book closes with a focus on the dreams, aspirations, and awakenings that accompany adolescence. This is a very important chapter because even though adolescence is a period of turmoil, a time of storm and stress, it is also a period of excitement, a time of "rebirth." The adolescent is filled with new ideas, sensations, feelings, talents, and visions of self and others. Adolescence is a time which, with the proper support and nurturance, can signify one's new start! It is in hopes of facilitating such support and nurturance that this book was written.

As is true of all that I do, many individuals have provided me with much support and guidance throughout the preparation of this text. While there are many youths, parents, and professionals who have shared their personnel experiences with me and who have, as such, provided the substance for much of what appears within this text, three pastoral counselors deserve special recognition: Diana Hoffman, Sr. Monica Bauer, and Rev. John Close. Their input, suggestions and editorial corrections have proven extremely valuable in helping to complete this text. Similarly, a special "thanks" goes to Bob Wicks, who as general editor provided valuable suggestions on style and content, and as my friend provided the encouragement and support I needed. Finally, to my wife, Karen, who has for years been *righting* my *writing,* a special thank you.

Chapter 1

Working with the Adolescent: A Special Challenge

Marked as a period of uncertainty, tension and rapid change, adolescence is a time of confusion and turmoil for both adolescents and for all those of significance to them—a point more than highlighted by their own voices. Amy,* age 17, is a "happy," achieving youth from a fine family. Attractive, intelligent, with good academic credentials and social skills, Amy may be expected to have "the world on a string." However, upon closer scrutiny, her view of self, and of her world does not seem as bright:

> "I don't know . . . it is so confusing—I have so many questions, so many decisions to make . . . I just don't know if I am even here sometimes. It's scary . . . Everything is changing . . . I am not sure I want to grow up . . . but I hate being so damn dependent, such a kid! The worst thing for me is that I am all alone in this . . . nobody really understands . . . it seems nobody really cares!"

The sentiments expressed, while more articulate than those of most other youths, are nonetheless shared reflections of what might be termed the universal condition of adolescence. Moreover, this is a condition which impacts parents as well as the youths themselves.

Mrs. H., the mother of John, age 15, epitomized the concern and sense of frustration experienced by many parents of adolescents:

> "Living with him lately is like being on a roller-coaster. I never know what to expect. At times he is my sweet, darling little boy, full of affection and concern . . .

*All names used are fictional; all case material is either a composite or developed to present a point.

7

happy-go-lucky . . . a real lover of life, but it seems that as soon as I let down my guard and begin to rejoice 'My son is home,' WHAM! Dr. Jekyll and Mr. Hyde. He becomes insolent, gruff. . . withdrawn. He refuses to communicate, stalks off to his room and locks himself into some private world. Yes it concerns me; it infuriates me; I guess what it really does is confuse me!"

Similar confusion and concern are manifested in parental statements such as:

"What's wrong with kids today . . . all they do is watch TV or hang on the phone with friends—what happened to the good old values of work, play, and family?"

"Education for this kid is a joke . . . if I had the opportunity the kids today have I certainly would be making use of it. They don't listen to teachers, they cut classes; they just aren't responsible."

"Fifty dollar jeans—crazy, you think. Well let me tell you, it's just the beginning. Their values are all messed up. 'I need this, that and the other thing; my hair has to be so, my clothes with the right labels.' If you want to see examples of screwed up values just talk to these kids!"

The adolescent—as reflected in these and the multitude of "other" experiences—is certainly an amalgam of conflicting moods and motives, habits and dreams. A source of constant frustration for the adults most concerned about their well-being, adolescents often appear to be in a state of flux. At times it seems they are the epitome of positive energy and innocent optimism; then at other times, they show themselves to be abruptly cynical and immobilized in worlds to which adults don't seem to have access.

Being neither a child nor an adult, these developmental "transients" often present values which seem somewhat distorted and attitudes which seem a bit bizarre. Marching to the beat of a different drummer, the adolescent seems always just out of step—a point of tension for both the adolescent and his/her parents. The particulars of each parent and adolescent interaction vary, depending on the "what," "why" and "who" involved. However, the exchange presented below highlights one all too consistent finding: parents and adolescents are quite often out of sync. It's as though they are speaking a foreign language . . . and truly dancing to a drummer of a different beat.

> *Son:* "My mom and dad think my dancing is barbaric, my music one step above racket, my friends crude, and all the things I like to do . . . a waste of time."

> *Dad:* "But they are . . . When I was your age . . ."

> *Son:* "See what I mean!"

> *Mom:* "We ask you what would you like to do, where would you like to go . . . and . . ."

> *Son:* "Yeah, you ask, but when I tell you I want to go 'hang' with my friends, or go to a concert . . . you FREAK."

> *Dad:* "Well, why can't you just spend time at home . . . be normal?"

And so it goes . . .

Adolescence is a period of development which places special demands on all involved in the nurturing of these youths. Parents, teachers, ministers, friends, and even the adolescents themselves who feel pushed to their limit and without further resource, often cry out for help. It is within this helping context that *everyone* involved formally and informally as youth ministers plays such an essential role.

Youth Ministry—An Opportunity for Everyone

Youth ministers* *are* in demand. The role is challenging, frustrating and painful, both by one's own perceived inability to "heal" the adolescent and their families and by one's sharing of their pain.

Viewed within the context of the Christian vision of service such suffering can serve as a basis for hope. Through a combination of "helping" skills and a commitment to spiritual values, it is possible not only to become touched by the adolescent but also to touch in a way that reaffirms. Through the use of genuine care and concern and the employment of "helping skills," the call is to facilitate their growth out of the crises and help heal their pain.

However, unlike other types of helping, this is a special ministry. Not only is there a need to provide strategies, directions and solutions to developmental concerns expressed but also there is an invitation to exercise a threefold ministry of the Church: kerygma, koinonia, and diakonia (Power, 1985). The task being faced then is to counsel in ways that symbolically, dynamically and verbally bring Christ to adolescents and their families.

Adolescents experiencing intense guilt and depression because of the conflicts they experience between their "values" and their sexual urges, for example, need to be guided, counseled and touched by a message of forgiveness. Bringing the word to youth in such a way that its power transforms them (i.e., kerygma) is essential to the healing process. In doing this, accepting our own "humanity" and weakness while simultaneously embracing the presence of grace will prove powerful elements in the healing process. Furthermore, adolescents estranged from their families isolated from their peers and self-absorbed in loneliness need to be touched by "community." Reaching out as "church"—i.e. welcoming youths as our brothers/sisters—and re-establishing the bonds of family are all reflections of the mission of *koinonia*.

Finally, as youth ministers the call is to both care and serve.

*The term "youth minister" is used here in its broadest context—namely, it refers to anyone working with adolescents (i.e., teachers, principals, parish clergy, youth workers, social service personnel, counselors, etc.), as well as, and maybe *especially*, parents who wish an insight into the stage called "adolescence" with all of its turmoils and its opportunities.

Faith without works is dead (Jas 2:17). It is in this ministering to adolescents and their families through availability, presence, and willingness to assist that one can reflect the third ministry of Church, *diakonia* (i.e. service).

Youth ministers are called—called to care . . . to serve . . . to give witness. However, as can be expected, enactment of such a ministry is far from an easy task, and it is with this in mind that the rest of this chapter and book is written.

From Resolving to Relating

One of the chief roadblocks to effective ministering to adolescents and their families is the ministers' well-meaning, often over-eager, over-zealous attempts to solve and resolve the problem with which they are presented. All too often when presented with cases at their doorstep, youth ministers are moved to intervene, to cure, to solve the problem with ready-made solutions and suggestions. The pain exhibited by adolescents and their families cries out for relief, thus instilling in helpers a great desire to swoop in to remove the suffering.

While the intentions are noble, the efforts are often less than effective. Consider my own encounter with Al. Al is 17 years old, an excellent student and up to this current "crisis" appears to have everything going for him. I saw Al after school, sitting on the church steps. I was struck first by his appearance of being intense in thought. As I approached him, I noticed that he had been crying. I sat down beside him and asked how he was doing. Following some brief social exchange, I pointed out that it looked as though something was worrying him, and as if I had tapped a magic button, he took my cue and began to relate his sad story.

With his senior prom less than a month away, Al came to the realization that his girlfriend of one year was not the girl he really wished to take. He had been asked to attend a prom by a second girl and had found the encounter to be especially gratifying.

Al was in turmoil. Torn by his desire to be faithful, he found it hard not to want to date this new friend. Further and somewhat more deeply, he was torn by his desire not to hurt anyone else—either his

new friend or his old friend. The only solution from his perspective
was to be destined to spend a prom (and a life) unhappy and unsat-
isfied.

Although this perspective seems distorted, discounting the severity of the situation would be an injustice. For Al, the moment
could hardly be more severe. Most of us would not mock or make
light of Al or his concerns. Nor would we act so impersonally as to
suggest that Al "flip a coin." However, it is just such messages which
are often conveyed by well-meaning suggestions. And so recognizing
Al's loss of perspective, we may miss the point and suggest:

"It is only puppy love—both she and you will get over it."

"Take one to the prom—and the other you could take out
on another night."

"Proms aren't what they are cracked up to be . . . no matter
what you do, in a week it won't even matter."

The suggestions appear reasonable and potentially quite
useful. However, such instant answers address the problem but
often fail to reflect the youth minister's real presence to the adolescent and his/her understanding of the youth's pain. As such, the
youth minister may find that his/her well-meaning suggestions are
met with apparent anger and resentment:

"You just don't understand. Nobody does. You think it's
funny . . . puppy love . . . it's supposed to be so easy . . .
I've heard it all! You don't care!"

A frustration for the youth minister is that oftentimes you *do*
have the answer. It must be remembered, however, that for this answer to prove effective, it must be heard, valued, incorporated and
enacted by the one we wish to help.

Helping is a human endeavor. It occurs only within the boundaries of a human encounter. As such what is needed is not merely
products (i.e., "solutions," "answers" and "techniques") but process—a process of supporting, of caring, of relating. This is not to im-

ply that intervening, teaching and directing are inappropriate. On the contrary, when working with the adolescent in crises you *must* be prepared to take action. What is suggested, however, is that such "prescriptive" activities must be couched within the context of a relationship. Prescription is effective only if it occurs after support and empathy have enabled the helper to truly enter into the adolescent's world of pain and dilemma.

Many helpers, youth ministers and parents rush into "doing" and "problem solving" with the adolescent without fully appreciating the essential value of the relationship to the "helping process." Developing a helping alliance with the adolescent is the essential, necessary—if not sufficient—condition for helping. The youth minister needs to attend to those factors which will facilitate the development of this relationship if he/she is truly to be helpful.

This is not easy, though. Building a helping relationship requires a shift in perspective. The roles to be emphasized, therefore, are that of listener rather than speaker, responder rather than initiator, and facilitator rather than director.

Roadblocks to Relating

Developing any relationship requires special care and nurturance. For those interested in developing a helping relationship with the adolescent, a number of special roadblocks and pitfalls exist and need to be considered.

Resisting Help

Seeking help and assistance with a problem requires acceptance of personal limits for self-reliance and the need for support. Adolescents will often view seeking and accepting help as antithetical to their own need for independence. Such an equation of help seeking with personal insufficiency and childish dependency must be removed if a helping relationship is to be developed.

Transference

The resistance to seeking and/or accepting help is often compounded by the tendency to transfer feelings, thoughts and expectations associated with prior adult relationships to this new encounter with the youth minister. In line with this, the youth minister is often placed in the role of parent. Then once having defined the youth minister within this authoritative role, adolescents may feel pressured to either succumb to the "good" parental figure or rebel against the "bad." Either reaction will interfere with the development of the helping relationship.

Generalizations

The attitudes and orientations of youth ministers can also serve as a major interference to the development of a helping relationship. Counselors, helpers, and youth ministers sometimes view the adolescent as a representative of a larger group. Thus they fail to see the individual person before them. Generalizing and overlooking the uniqueness of each youth may result in failure to define the youth's unique concerns or in assigning unhelpful labels such as "adolescent rebellion," "search for identity," etc. Therefore pat answers and clichéd advice may be offered to what the adolescent feels to be a unique, personal tragedy. This will only set the stage for further distancing on the part of the adolescent because of his/her feeling that he/she is not understood.

Countertransference

In addition to the danger of generalization, the helper needs to be aware of the possible negative influence of "countertransference." Adolescence is a period of pain from which the youth counselor was neither immune nor totally free. Because adolescence may have been a problematic period for certain youth ministers, they may find that the behavior which this particular adolescent exhibits seems to provoke a great deal of pain, anxiety, confusion and negative feelings within them. Youth ministers who are uncomfortable with their own sexuality, for example, may engage in projection as to what the "kids of today" are doing. Those who are questioning their own religious values and commitment may try to impose a rigid, moralistic view and proselytized solutions onto the adolescent's concerns. Further, those for whom dealing with authority figures is an unresolved area of conflict may have difficulty with the rebellious tendencies in adolescence. Under such conditions the helper may perceive problems with sexuality, values or authority where none exists or might even identify with the adolescent's acting out behavior and encourage it. The process of developing an effective helping relationship is open to a great deal of possible interference. It is difficult but not impossible. Still a therapeutic alliance can be established if the young person can be assisted to feel that he or she is sincerely, accepted and accurately understood.

Facilitating an Alliance

Adolescents in crisis do not turn to youth workers in order to have another adult "tell them what to do." Adolescents are seeking an ally. They, like their parents, are in crises, in pain, and they seek support and understanding. It is this support and understanding that rests as the cornerstone of the helping process. The task then is to give evidence of this support and understanding.

Effective youth ministers, effective helpers, will be those who give witness to the basic, intrinsic value of the person by their own manifestation of a warm, accepting, genuine and respectful attitude for the adolescent or parent with whom they work. Providing such "witness" can be facilitated by a clear understanding of the elements of acceptance, warmth, respect and genuineness. As such, each of these qualities is more fully discussed below.

Acceptance

Adolescents in turmoil come from a world of actual or perceived rejection. Rejection by self and by their significant others (e.g., parents, teachers, friends) is often the primary reason for seeking support. Effectiveness in helping youths will depend largely on an ability to create a climate of mutual acceptance.

True acceptance demands a refusal to exercise control over adolescents or to dictate how they should or shouldn't respond. The temptation to impose roles or norms of behavior on adolescents should be avoided in order to let adolescents be who they are, at this particular moment, while facilitating their growth, to be the "who" they wish to be.

This acceptance requires laying aside both formal status and informal social roles which may interfere with an open relationship. Roles such as "teacher-student," "pastor-parishioner," and "confessor-penitent" will impose stringent demands and limitations on an open relationship. The adolescent with sexual conflicts and concerns may wish to discuss these with Jim, Janice, or Mr. S, but may feel it is "wrong" to discuss them with Deacon Jim, Sister Janice, or Father Smith. Approaching the youth from roles of authority and power will not only restrict the topics and areas for discussion but may create expectations which are destructive to the experience of an open, caring relationship. Should adolescents feel that sharing these concerns becomes a confession of weakness they may begin to expect absolution rather than resolution.

It is important to be guided by the "here and now" of the interaction rather than being controlled by "a priori" role expectations. Accepting youths as they are rather than as they are supposed to be will allow both, the adolescent and the youth minister, to revel in the glory of uniqueness and specialness of this moment.

In attempting to maintain this sense of acceptance, it may be helpful for the youth minister to remember that such acceptance ultimately comes from God, and not from the youth minister. By the virtue of creation, this youth *is* acceptable.   .

However, all acceptance does not imply absolute, wholesale approval of what is *said* or *done* by the adolescent—or parent, for that matter. Such wholesale acceptance or approval of another is often a way of expressing radical non-involvement or non-concern (Egan, 1977). If a youth is really cared for, then there is a need to extend yourself in hopes of educating, motivating or encouraging that adolescent to grow. To stimulate and encourage change and movement from destructive patterns is a reflection of personal acceptance and concern.

Even when you have intentions of changing adolescents' way of thinking, feeling or acting, true acceptance of them requires actively allowing adolescents the freedom *not* to change, if that be their desire. Therefore, even if the recommendations are excellent, the temptation to demand or expect implementation must be avoided. The exception to this would be the case of intervention in suicidal or homicidal activities.

Non-Possessive Warmth and Respect

In addition to acceptance, the adolescent needs to feel "prized" and valued. Quite often the adolescent brings to an interpersonal encounter feelings of negative worth and minimal self-esteem. The youth's journey to a helper's doorstep has generally been accompanied by failure, disappointment and evidence of inadequacy. For the adolescent, self-worth and value is often conditional.

The adolescent sees self as valued, prized, respected only under the "conditions" of producing good grades, having the right clothes, or fulfilling another's expectations. These conditions of worth are generally lacking in the experience of troubled adolescents. Coming to this encounter, adolescents will reflect their sense of worthlessness by stating "I'm failing"; "I don't have a girlfriend"; "My mom's furious with me." Behind these statements is the implied negative value of self that "I am a failure"; "I am unlikeable"; "I am a disappointment to all who care."

The adolescent operating under this orientation of conditional worth needs to experience and understand the basic *unconditional, non-possessive* basis of worth. Unconditional, non-possessive warmth reflects a deep non-evaluative respect for the person's thoughts, feelings, and wishes. "Prizing" another is a reflection of a belief that the individual, endowed with natural gifts and talents, is created in the image and likeness of God.

To respect others requires a true appreciation of and value for them because they are human beings, special creations of God. One simple way in which this can be manifested is through a willingness to provide adolescents who come for help with your uninterrupted, undiverted time and attention. Being present to the adolescent in need rather than turning to the more "serious" and "pressing" concerns of things (e.g., marking papers, preparing the homily, etc.) provides evidence for a special valuing of this young person. In light of this, it would perhaps be more helpful to adolescents to refuse to open the door to them in some cases rather than to invite them into an exchange marked by inattentiveness and distraction.

While unconditional positive regard for the person is essential, unconditional approval of all they do is neither appropriate nor desirable. Taking a cue from Christ's ability to love the sinner while hating the sin, clearly distinguishing an evaluation of adolescents' behavior from the existential love held for them as persons must be learned and exhibited. Unlike Christ, however, we will often find it hard, if not nearly impossible, to look beyond the behavior which is presented. It is easy to be distracted from prizing individuals, as it is natural to fall into the habit of valuing them for what they do or don't do. Showing the adolescent approval based on his/her willingness to follow recommendations or to act the "right way" not only interferes with the message of unconditional love, but also promotes a continuation of the adolescent's own process of conditional valuing. At those times when it is difficult to look beyond the conditions of this or that youth to see the underlying valued human, other professionals should be called upon for support, in the form of consultation and/or referral of the adolescent.

Genuineness

One final ingredient to building a supportive, understanding, helping relationship is the maintenance and manifestation of *genuineness*. In an eagerness as helpers to "do it correctly" there is a temptation to "put on" care and concern, as one might put on a role in a play. Caring, supporting, and loving another cannot be put on. All of the previous discussion of facilitative conditions is for nought if the helper is not, first and foremost, authentic and genuine in the relationship.

Attaining and maintaining such genuineness is not an easy process. We have been trained to take on roles, and with them to assume behaviors which at any one time may be less than genuine. The teacher, who because of personal concerns would rather be home on the night of the PTA, has been taught to put on the best face and provide a pleasant, professional front to the parents that evening. The minister, angered and concerned about the financial demands of his church, knows that he is expected to smile, be pleasant, and repress the strong negative feelings when talking with Mr. and Mrs. H, two of his generous contributors. These and other "roles" do serve a social purpose. It is neither appropriate nor necessarily helpful to surrender all masks or roles used in daily social encounters.

But the helping relationship is special. It demands honest, role-free, genuine exchange.

Genuineness involves responding authentically in both a negative and a positive manner (Carkhuff, 1969). Authenticity or genuineness within the helping relationship is achieved only when the youth minister is free of roles and rigid formulas. The youth minister who is genuine is open as opposed to defensive, is real as opposed to phony. When authentic and genuine, interacting in an integrated fashion becomes possible. Likewise, feelings, thoughts and behaviors all reflect the same reality. Being congruent in words, expression, tone, action and feelings is a clear sign of genuineness. Expressing and admitting discomfort or even disappointment and discouragement when they are experienced is more facilitative than attempting to always present a positive, encouraged, relaxed image, when such is not the case. As effective helpers, trying to remain nondefensive and avoiding retreating into the facade of a professional role is a must. In asking the adolescent to be open and real to you, there is a need for the helper to reflect the same!

Concluding Thoughts

Working with youth and their families is both renewing and draining. Along with the "highs" which accompany successful interventions, there will also be the inevitable lows. There will be times when you do not know what else you can do to open the hearts, to open the ears, and to provide the needed vision for the youth in trouble. At these times of peak frustration and exhaustion, taking heart and receiving a renewed spirit from reflecting upon the ministry of Christ is essential.

When pushed to the limit, solace and encouragement can be found in the parable regarding a widow depositing a few coins in the treasury. In this parable, Jesus was reported to have said that she was more blessed than those who had given out of their abundance. "I tell you this," he said. "This poor widow has given more than any of them, for those others who have given had more than enough, but she, with less than enough, has given all she had to live on." (Lk

21:1–4). Clearly Jesus is saying: Assess your values, your priorities, and your gifts and continue to give what you are able to give. Most often when feeling the most drained, a reflection on one's gifts and values will open new springs of energy and renewal of spirit. Such a message is not only for the helper but also for the tired, hapless parent—and the desperate, resolute youth.

Once renewed, one may still feel at a loss as to what to do, what to say. Again, the actions and words of Jesus are there as guidance. The Gospel of Mark (1:40–45), for example, provides a clear reminder of what one's duty as helper and healer should be. Reflecting on Christ's cleansing of the leper, Mark noted that Christ first gave his attention to the person in need; he affirmed the leper's beauty and worth unconditionally and responded authentically and freely. Not knowing what to say or what to do is an experience everyone encounters. Being mindful at these times of the model of helping reflected by Christ is worthwhile. Being attentive, affirming the person's intrinsic worth and extending oneself genuinely and authentically—this is what's needed. To heal, to help, to serve, one must respond in faith and love.

References

Carkhuff, R.R. *Helping and Human Relations* (2 vols.). New York: Holt, Rinehart and Winston, 1969.

Egan, G. *You and Me*. Monterey: Brooks/Cole, 1977.

Power, F.C. "The Role of the Pastoral Counselor in the Primary and Secondary School." In Wicks, R., Parsons, R. and Capps, D. *Clinical Handbook of Pastoral Counseling*. Mahwah: Paulist Press, 1985, 406–424.

Recommended Readings

D'Augelli, A., Danish, S.J., Hauer, A.L. and Conter, J.J. *Helping Skills: A Basic Training Program*. New York: Human Science Press, 1980.

Egan, G. *The Skilled Helper*. Monterey: Brooks/Cole, 1975.

Wicks, R. *Helping Others*. New York: Gardner Press, 1982.

Wicks, R. and Parsons, R. D. *Counseling Strategies and Intervention Techniques for the Human Services.* New York: Longman Press, Inc., 1984.

Van Ornum, W. and Mordock, J. B. *Crisis Counseling with Children and Adolescents.* New York: Continuum, 1984.

Chapter 2

Adolescence: Storm and Stress

The adolescent is certainly a bewildering amalgam of conflicting moods and motives, habits and dreams. One noted scholar defined adolescents as lacking in self-constraint, fickle, insolent, irascible and apt to get carried away by their impulses. They were presented as being an extremist and idealistic; if they commit a fault it is always on the side of excess and exaggeration.

Those who feel uniquely "plagued" by troubled adolescents, and the adolescents themselves who feel singularly doomed, may take heed from the above description, knowing that it was originally cited by Aristotle, over 2,300 years ago. While taking a unique form in the 1980's, adolescence is a developmental phase experienced by each and every generation in their journey toward maturity.

The term "adolescence" is derived from the Latin *adolescere* meaning "to grow to maturity." In this sense of growth, adolescence is a *process* rather than a period, a process of evolving from child to adult. The questioning, experimenting, challenging and finding which mark this period of development have as their bases the desire for self-discovery and understanding of the *ultimate meaning*. As with any such period or process of development, adolescence can be viewed as an appointed time—a time when the specific developmental issues to be addressed come to bear. The task and search is mysterious and momentous. It is a journey to relish, knowing that God has "made everything appropriate to its time" (Eccl 3:11).

For those called to be a part of this "appointed time," the calling and responsibility is to facilitate this process of growth and development so that each youth may be better able to respond to Jesus' invitation. In order to carry out this ministry the experience of adolescents and those factors contributing to the success or hindrance of their development needs to be understood. The current chapter will attempt to provide such an informational basis by discussing the varied biological, sociological and psychological factors impacting the adolescent experience.

A Journey—Stormy and Stressful

As previously noted, consideration and discussion of the adolescent has a history as classical as the works of Aristotle. However, real attention to this stage of development began early in 1880's with G. Stanley Hall's "child study movement." Hall presented his observations about adolescents in a paper published in the *Princeton Review* in 1882, entitled "The Moral and Religious Training of Children." In this presentation, Hall introduced us to the concept of adolescence as a period of storm and stress, a period characterized by a lack of emotional steadiness, violent impulses, unreasonable conduct, lack of enthusiasm and sympathy, a period in which the previous selfhood is broken up and a new individual is in process of being born, peculiarly susceptible to external influences.

The turmoil noted by Hall—the same experienced by all who have developed through adolescence—was attributed to the vast degree of biological change and the resultant stress found in this period of development. Skeletal growth, hormonal imbalance and emergence of new and wonderous traits (e.g., new capabilities for thinking in the abstract, sexual feelings, etc.) had, according to this position, manifested themselves in the form of the viability of mood and conduct which is so characteristic of the adolescent.

From such a biologically based position, the *prescription* for the youth, their parents and the youth minister would be simply: "Hold on! Sit it out! Time will eventually bring the adolescent back into normal balance." While such a position removes adolescents and those dealing with them from responsibility for contributing to, if not creating, this condition, it also places everyone involved in a helpless "wait and see" posture.

The biological, fixed position on the adolescent experience, however, was not maintained by all who studied or worked with adolescence. Margaret Mead, for example, in her *Coming of Age in Samoa* (1928), became one of the more verbal opponents of the biological position held by Hall. Dr. Mead attempted to demonstrate the role culture and social factors played in the creation and perhaps amelioration of the storm and stress characteristic of the adolescent period.

Mead's observation along with the subsequent years of study and research has led most theorists to view adolescence as a period resulting from the interactive influences of biological and social forces. From this interactional view, adolescence is viewed as a time when internal drives and desires attempt to find expression within the confines, constraints and external requirements of society. It is a time of testing and learning. It is a time of uncertain change and frustration. It is a time of experimentation, discovery and growth. It is a time when the adolescent attempts to answer the questions "Who am I?" and "Who am I to be?"

The Question of Identity

Ask a six year old child to answer the question "Who are you?" and you might get a response such as: "I'm Jonathan. I'm six years old and I am in first grade. I like to play soccer, Star Wars and G.I. Joe. My friend is Jon. I live in Westtown and I'd like to be an astronaut." Similarly, and with as much ease as that exhibited by the six year old, his father might note: "I am a psychologist, married with three children, and I work at a local college. I like to play tennis and lately I am getting into working with my hands. I like to write. I need to lose weight and am looking forward to a sabbatical."

Adults and children tend to respond to the question of identity with the same type of response. "Self," for these two groups, is often defined using referents which include "biological or physical traits," "social roles and status," and personal evaluations and reflections on "qualities and aspirations."

Why then is it so difficult and obviously so painful for the adolescent to respond to the same identity issue and question of "Who am I?" Unlike the other two groups, adolescents find that their referents, their anchors—for example, their biological self (body, sex-type, etc.), their social status and roles (first grader, or psychologist) and their self-perception of qualities and aspirations—are not only unclear, but are not even stable. Adolescents experience their bodies and their social world as being turned inside out, changing uncontrollably and unpredictably, a condition of flux and uncertainty.

One youth named Jacob with whom I was working helped clarify the "crisis" nature of this issue by sharing the following dream. He wrote:

> "I had a dream . . . no, not a dream . . . a nightmare. I saw myself waking up and found myself in someone else's body. It was unrecognizable. It was as if I were trapped in some type of shell. There were internal feelings and sensations which were occurring which were alien to me. The body seemed to change hourly and I had no control over it. I didn't even have a sense of its direction or the ultimate outcome. It was as if I had absolutely no control!
>
> My friends, family—they all changed. Not physically . . . but the way they treated me, the way they looked at me. They changed all of the rules. Sometimes I had to do this or that and other times I was forbidden from doing those very same things. There didn't seem to be any rhyme or reason for the rules imposed on me. Again, I felt like a victim in a strange world, with no control. But the scariest thing of all was that even those things that I valued, that I cherished, that seemed to be so much a natural part of who I was, began to change. I felt differently about my family, the rules of society, religion, rights and wrongs—everything needed to be re-examined.
>
> It was as if I was someone else, but I had no idea who. I didn't know who I was or where I was going or what was important, anymore. I wanted to scream, to run, to just ESCAPE!"

The above dream was not only a horrifying nightmare but an almost unbearable condition for one like Jacob who perceived himself as living through it. The confusion, turmoil and crises reflected by the dreamer are what is experienced by many adolescents as part of their "normal" development as they attempt to answer the question "Who am I?" The biological, social and psycho-emotional points of reference typically employed in anchoring one's identity are all in a state of flux, a state of change—and because of that the adolescent oftentimes feels overwhelmed and out of control.

Better understanding of the actual and somewhat predictable changes which the adolescent is experiencing and the potential effect such changes may have on the adolescent is necessary to understand the adolescent experience so that sharing that understanding with adolescents and their parents becomes possible. And it is this shared understanding that serves as a basis for providing the support and care needed by the adolescent during this period of storm and stress.

Self as Body Image

One of the first reference points for self-identity is one's body image. "I'm a boy," "I'm tall," "I'm strong," are all beginning reflection of the "I" which we all seek to identify.

An immense, somewhat mysterious journey, the transformation of the child into an adult starts with pubescence. The "whats" and the "hows" are not completely understood, but the journey is a continual one and the impact is plainly visible. The body image with which the child had become so clearly identified undergoes radical change during adolescence. How many of us have said goodbye to our students, or youth group, at the end of an academic year only to return in the fall to find what first appears to be a group of strangers. The boys look as though they have grown a foot and the "girls" are now women.

This *growth spurt,* which can occur as early as seven and one-half, most typically occurs around the age of eleven for girls and thirteen for boys (Tanner, 1972). In addition to the skeletal growth, hormonal activity will start to manifest itself in the development of the primary and secondary sexual characteristics which identify the mature male (i.e., mature sperm, ejaculation, deeper voice, facial hair, etc.) and the mature female (mature ova, menses, breast development, etc.).

The changes in one's physical appearance are often experienced by the adolescent, much like that described in Jacob's dream, as being an uncontrollable nightmare.

"I go to bed, after looking in the mirror and saying 'not bad' . . . only to wake up in the morning with pimples, weird looking marks, funny looking breasts, etc."

"I hate it. Everybody is getting whiskers. Why not me!"

"I refuse to go swimming. Everybody looks at me just because of these dumb breasts. A guy's not supposed to be flabby like this!"

"Look at me. I'm taller than all my boyfriends . . . a real Amazon!"

It is as if the adolescent's body is erupting, changing without any possible control and without any predictable outcome.

It is hard for adults to truly appreciate this sense of lack of control and direction. Somewhat mercifully most adults have blocked it out of their memories. As an adult, the body is changing, but at a much slower rate. For example, if one wanted to attain a specific goal, such as to lose weight, an adult can develop a reasonable strategy to achieve the desired outcome. There is a recognition that changing one's body takes time and work. For the adolescent, however, it is not so simple. Things seem to change on their own, sometimes overnight. They may know where they would like to go with their "body self"—to lose weight, develop bigger (smaller) breasts or more muscles, to be taller, to have more (less) body hair, etc.—but they are often without reasonable plans or methods for getting there. Further, even when the plan appears reasonable, their bodies often appear to operate outside of any control on their part.

"I watch my diet and clean my face but I still have pimples!"

"I work out like the other guys and watch what I eat, but I still have flabby breasts!"

The importance of these various biological changes lies in the fact that the adolescent's changing body and body image provides the basis from which self-concept and self-worth often take shape. With such an unpredictable, ever changing, and oftentime undesirable body image, it is understandable why adolescents may experience concern and confusion over the question of "Who am I?" and in turn devote so much time and energy to attending to their body and their bodily images. Consider Sally, a sixteen year old with whom I was working. She called me one evening hysterically. The prom was that evening and her face was "riddled with pimples." She was "ugly" and her life was about to be ruined—all because of "this curse of adolescence!"

Granted, as an adult I may feel that Sally's reaction was extreme, but the feelings she disclosed were both painful and concerning. While I saw it as a matter of simple biological change, a change which is only transient and not core to the issue of "who she was" or "how beautiful she truly was," for Sally the pimples and the ugliness were HER.

It is important that you begin to appreciate the "crisis" nature and significance of these experiences for the adolescent. Attempting to argue with Sally about the "beauty which is intrinsic" or even attempting to demonstrate the imperceptible nature of the pimple not only will prove unproductive but may demonstrate to her another adult's insensitivity and lack of empathy for her. And so, replacing a comment such as "Don't be silly; it's no big deal," which seems true, with one such as "I guess that does bother you," may bring the adolescent and the concerned adult into a closer problem solving alliance. Rather than spending time and energy arguing the philosophical nature of beauty, forces can be joined now to reduce the negative effects of this "ghastly looking thing." The reaction "It's really a darn shame. Your hair looks super and your gown is beautiful. I wonder how we could hide that pimple," will most obviously prove more effective than simply saying, "It's no big deal. You're exaggerating the whole thing. Go and get dressed!"

Sensitivity to the "crisis" nature of these changes is necessary in order to be better able to empathize with the adolescent. In addition, assisting the adolescent's parents to gain that same sensitivity and empathy for the adolescent's condition is also important. This gained sensitivity will help them all to better cope with the day to day emotional/social crises that often result.

Take, for example, the parent who finds the family in upheaval and in constant conflict because his son is always in the bathroom. "He spends at least two hours each morning trying to get his hair just right." Such a parent may find it a bit more tolerable and resolvable if he is able to more accurately and empathetically understand it as his son's attempt to identify and reconcile his own self-worth, prior to placing his image on the evaluation line of his peers. While the inability to use the bathroom will still prove to be an annoyance, it will now be one in which the concerns of the adolescent will be viewed as legitimate and for which a mutually satisfying solution will be sought.

In addition to understanding both the changes and the personal impact such changes have on the adolescent, sensitivity to one's own reaction to these changes is also essential. Consider the kidding and ribbing the adolescent male receives as he attempts to answer in class or respond to his parents, only to hear a strange, cracking and squeaking voice emerge from his mouth. Surely it is embarrassing enough without the adult making it a point of humor. Or consider the more intense stress of the late maturer who fears that he will always be the "shrimp," both "hairless" and "sexually inadequate," and who finds himself being teased by an adult about "the fuzz on his lip."

The biological clock is in full swing for the adolescent. These changes are mysterious, unpredictable, exciting and often traumatizing. It is a time for providing the adolescent with accurate information about his or her body and bodily changes. It is a time to demonstrate an accurate, empathetic understanding of the importance of these changes. It is a time to support and extend tolerance to the adolescent during this period of change.

Self as Social Entity

While all individuals of all environments go through the same forms of biological change, the resulting impact and level of stress varies significantly culture to culture, family to family, child to child.

As Margaret Mead first noted, the severe stress of adolescence appears more symptomatic of industrialized cultures than of more primitive cultures. Her explanation pointed to the important role played by the "rite of passage" for these cultures. Such a rite clearly defined the point of demarcation between childhood and adulthood. Further, the specific rite, once completed, brought with it all of the rights and responsibilities of adulthood. Such a "rite" moved the child from the secure position of childhood to the security of a clear, well-defined role as an adult.

In the "civilized" industrialized cultures, no such rite of passage exists. Adolescents find themselves moved from childhood with the biological awakening of puberty, but are almost never sure as to when they move into adulthood. At various times demands of adult-status are placed upon adolescents, without the parallel rights and freedoms. Living a life of ambiguity and uncertainty is clearly stressful and emotionally disruptive. The more the ambiguity, be it within the culture at large, or within a particular family, the more the stress and emotional upheaval it will create. Messages assumed to be so clear often are the height of ambiguity. "Act your age" is often the cry of parents to their daughter demanding that she "wash that silly makeup off her face." However, those same parents will find that same phrase to be a useful means of telling their daughter, "Grow up and take more responsibility for your life." Similarly, the adolescent who attempts to follow his parents' directive, "Learn to stand on your own two feet. Make your own decisions. Don't blindly follow the crowd," will find that the directive results in conflict and strife at home if he attempts to challenge his parents' rules and stand on his own two feet or question rather than blindly follow.

Perhaps the often unpredictable and somewhat emotionally unstable behavior of adolescents can be more clearly appreciated as a response to the social position in which adults place them. Adolescents are inconsistent and unstable because adults place them in the inconsistent, unstable position of an ambiguous adult-child social role—a position, a role which experiences inconsistent demands and expectations and unpredictable consequences. Because of this ambiguity of social roles, adolescents are inclined to shyness, sensitivity and aggressiveness to mask their insecurity. Not knowing what is expected of them, the adolescent is concerned about "messing up" and looking foolish.

Adolescents can be assisted by helping them to define and establish their own social position. They and their parents need help to clarify and identify the specific rights and duties the youth may expect to be assigned. Further, efforts also need to be made so that parents may be helped to begin to incorporate "consistency" in the demands they place on their adolescents and the "freedoms" that they allow. It is through this increased clarity and consistency of the adolescent "social role" that they will begin to develop a mature, responsible social self-image.

Concluding Thoughts

Books and articles, of both a popular and a professional nature, which deal with the subject of adolescence disagree widely on the precise meaning of the term. Adolescence has been treated as a specific span of years, a stage of development, a subculture, a state of mind or a combination of these concepts. The confusion manifested even in these attempts at definition may be the best reflection of the uniqueness of adolescence. Adolescence is clearly a state of confusion and turmoil.

Adolescents are searching for a way out of the chaos, the confusion and the ambiguity of the adolescent experience. Any role which assists them in answering the question "Who am I?" is an important one—one that is indeed worth being involved in as Christians.

References

Hall, G.S. "The Moral and Religious Training of Children." In *Princeton Review,* January 1882, pp. 26–48.

Mead, M. *Coming of Age in Samoa.* New York: W. Morrow and Company, 1928.

Tanner, J.M. "Sequence, Tempo and Individual Variation in Growth and Development of Boys and Girls Ages 12 to 16." In J. Kagan and R. Coles (eds.), *12–16: Early Adolescence.* New York: W.W. Norton, 1972 (pp. 1–24).

Recommended Readings

Ginott, H.G. *Between Parent & Teenager.* New York: Avon Books, 1969.

Hill, J.P. *Understanding Early Adolescence: A Framework.* Carrboro: Center for Early Adolescence, University of North Carolina, 1980.

Kitwood, J. *Disclosures to a Stranger: Adolescent Values in an Advanced Industrial Society.* London: Routledge and Kegan Paul, 1980.

Offer, D., Ostrov, E. and Howard, I.K. *The Adolescent: A Psychological Self-Portrait.* New York: Basic Books, 1981.

Shelton, C.M. *Adolescent Spirituality.* Chicago: Loyola University Press, 1983.

Strommen M. and Strommen, A.I. *Five Cries of Parents.* New York: Harper & Row, 1985.

Chapter 3

================

Communications

"I don't know what has happened . . . we used to be so close. We could talk about everything; now she never has time for me."

"Communicate! You've got to be kidding. How do you communicate with someone who just grunts?"

"I just don't understand. What do they want? If you try to talk with them they ignore you or get angry. If you let them alone, they say you don't care."

It is commonly held that much of the trouble between the generations is due to their inability or unwillingness to communicate. The above statements, interestingly, could have been made by either parent or child. It appears that the problems with communication and the experienced gap in understanding are felt as equally painful on both sides of the youth-age line. Parents have for a long time cried the lament that their adolescent "no longer talks to them." Similarly, adolescents are quick to remind us that the adults in their life refuse to *listen*, or never have the time for them, or are too quick with the answers, always interrupting, never permitting them the time to explain or present their view.

Problems with intergenerational communication are certainly not unique to the 1980's. The adolescent has a long-standing history of communication blocking. Communicating through the use of cryptic terms such as "tough," "cool," "nerd," "bad," etc., along with a reliance on non-verbal channels of communication (hand gestures, signals, emblems, clothes, etc.), was as evident in the 1930's and 1940's as they are today. The split in adolescent-adult communication is both normative and quite predictable. The shift in communication style and focus is the natural accompaniment to the adolescent's drive toward adult status.

As adolescents seek to increase their independence they actively attempt to exclude the "other" generation from their lives. In order to increase the integrity of their own "generation," adolescents strive for increased privacy not only by spending more time away from their family (e.g., with friends, in their room, etc.), but also by withholding information. The strong need to develop their own social bonding and the development of reference groups outside of the family force them to develop new styles of relating and communicating. Although the initial stages of this shift often generate minor conflicts (regarding hair, music, missed dinners or attendance at family outings, etc.), such conflict need not continue nor need it be a signal for the discontinued contact and understanding within the family. Therefore, there is a need to sharpen your communication skills so as to facilitate an understanding of adolescents and in turn their understanding of themselves. Similarly, there is a need to be able to *share* an understanding of the principles of facilitative communication with the adolescents' parents as well. Through this sharing these parents can be better prepared to understand their adolescent sons or daughters and in turn be better able to bridge their own communication gap.

A Time To Send . . . A Time To Receive

Adults often assume (and sometimes rightfully so) that they know more than their adolescent counterparts. From this vantage point adults poise themselves ready to give information, direction, advice and guidance. Armed with a barrage of questions, confrontations and various verbal probes, intended "rap" sessions often appear more like advice-giving meetings or intensive interrogation. "Where were you? Why didn't you call? Talk to me. What has happened to us?" Rapid-fire questions, with little pause for response, often machine gun out at adolescents, eliciting from them a protective, defensive grunt, grumble or deafening silence. Even in those instances when such interrogations are avoided, many parents, teachers and youth ministers, in their attempt to "communicate" and "relate" with the adolescents, find themselves taking center stage. These adults often end up providing lectures or personal monologues, giving the rights and wrongs, the "way to do it," or simply controlling the time for their own personal disclosure. While such direction, guidance and disclosure may at times prove helpful, what youths request and what they certainly need most is to be listened to. However, having said this, there still remains a problem as is illustrated by the following oft heard remark by parents and youth workers alike: "Listen! You've got to be kidding. I would give anything if I could listen to these kids. They won't talk to me. I can't get a thing out of them. They just *will not communicate!*"

I am sure that the sentiment expressed by the youth worker in the above statement is echoed by many teachers, youth ministers, counselors and parents. This sentiment is not only common but quite valid, if a narrow definition of "communication" is used. If communication is seen as only those social times wherein the adolescent sits before adults and quite politely and mannerly articulates his/her needs, wants, desires, thoughts and aspirations, then surely this would be a rarity. If, however, communication is defined as that process of sending information from one individual to another, then it must be agreed that communication occurs all of the time.

Communication occurs not just with words but through a variety of channels and forms. Silence, for example, speaks quite loudly, as in the situation where the offended girlfriend refuses to speak at dinner. Clearly the silence communicates significantly to her partner. Similarly, messages are conveyed by the adolescent who suddenly takes to his room, the youth who refuses to go to the dance or the daughter who, in a rare gesture of recognition, touches her father's shoulder as she enters from a date. Each of these youths is communicating and attempting to send information to his or her intended receiver. The question for the concerned receiver is: "What is the message I am to receive? How do I interpret these actions?"

It is clear that while communication can be completely effective, misinterpreted, or inadequate, it cannot be non-existent. Thus a major source of difficulty with communicating with the adolescent lies not so much in their "refusal" to *send* information as it is in the adult's inability to adequately *receive* and understand the information sent. It is not sufficient to simply listen with one's ears, but rather there is a need to employ all of the channels of reception in trying to understand the adolescent. Listening with one's ears, eyes, and hearts—the very being—is a skill which does not come easily, but one which is essential to develop on the road to being truly effective in one's efforts to understand the adolescent.

Listening: Setting the Stage

It is not only essential that those working with the adolescent practice the tenets of good listening, but it is also imperative that they "teach" parents to employ the same methods. Good listening, be it with one's own children, or with a spouse or friends, serves as the foundation stone for genuine communication. It is a skill not to be hoarded, but to be fostered in all with whom one comes into contact. However, in order to become an effective listener, the encounter must first be approached with a proper mind set and orientation and with a sense of total presence to the other.

Presence as Time and Ear

Communication and message reception is not an easy task. It demands our attention, time and energy. It requires our "presence" to the other.

Providing half an ear, such as is the case when a person is in the middle of a task to which he/she wishes to return or when there is a consciousness of time constraints (i.e., meeting a deadline of another project) or when being distracted by other personal concerns, may do more harm to the understanding of the adolescent and the development of a meaningful relationship, than would the rescheduling of the session. No one feels heard if, while talking with another about something particularly exciting or important in one's life, the "listener" is simultaneously paying attention to the TV, the typewriter, or the performance of some other chore. Under these circumstances not only does the receiver fail to completely and effectively receive the full impact of the person's intended message—as evidenced by their clichéd response of "Oh, that's nice" or "What a shame!"—but he/she clearly communicates a disinterest in the message and perhaps in the person. In an instance like this, the adolescent seeking affirmation will be quick to note such inattention and quicker to conclude that it is hopeless and useless to attempt further communication. It is important, therefore, to find the time when the energy can be devoted to the youth and vice versa. This does not mean that one needs to find a day or an hour; often it is only five or ten minutes that is required. What is essential is that the time which is devoted to the youth is exactly that, time just for one another.

Presence as Posture and Physical Attending

In addition to allocating the time and the energy for adolescents, "presence" must also be demonstrated to them by maintaining proper attention. Attending or "being with" another can be facilitated by the adoption of a specific physical posture or stance. Gerard Egan (1977) discussed the importance of body orientation in setting the stage, physically, for attending and receiving information. Egan suggested that facilitative attending behavior could be characterized as face-to-face, straight body orientation, opened in body posture, with a comfortable, relaxed, slight forward lean and the maintenance of eye contact. The literature is abundant in the support of the effectiveness of such a body position in increasing the accuracy of information received as well as increasing the perception of the listener's warmth and receptivity.

It appears that by simply taking a S.O.L.E.R. (straight, open, lean, eye, relaxed) position, one's own reception is facilitated by "opening" up all of one's channels of information reception. It also signals to the youth via body language that one is in complete attendance and presence to him/her. Thus, this posture encourages disclosure and continued communication.

The relative simplicity and perhaps obvious nature of the S.O.L.E.R. stance leads many to give lip service to its value: "Oh, yeah, I knew that," while at the same time failing to employ it in their daily communication practice. To emphasize the potential value of this very simple body orientation to youth workers, parents or adolescents who may feel that it is a silly game, I have employed the following exercise.

I ask the youth minister, parent or youth to sit down in front of me and describe for me the nature of his or her job (or any such personally relevant topic, such as interests, hobbies, feelings about something, etc.). I take up a SOLER position. As he or she begins to speak, however, I start to deviate from this "facilitative posture." Slowly, I will begin to rotate my body, clockwise, away from the speaker, starting first with a simple head turn, then shoulders and trunk, until my entire body becomes oriented away from the speaker. It is rare that I get to a point where my back is turned to the speaker (i.e., 180 degree rotation) before the speaker will stop talking and, perhaps somewhat annoyed, ask me why I am not looking or listening to him or her. While the point of turning one's back on the speaker is extreme, it does emphasize the fact that when there is no eye contact one feels less than attended to by the other person.

As the exercise continues, I will have speakers continue to communicate and then modify each of the other variables, taking each to an extreme in order to highlight their significance in facilitating or hindering (in their absence) communication. Thus, I will oftentimes begin in an open body position and, as they speak, begin to close up my body, by crossing my arms, then legs, then pulling my knees up and head down to my chest. The reaction from the speakers is that they generally feel that I am not attending or that perhaps they said something wrong. The speakers will generally note that my closed body style inhibits their ongoing communication.

Without belaboring the point it is my hope that one can imagine how modifying the other aspects of our SOLER position (e.g., leaning further back, away from the speaker, avoiding eye contact, sitting quite tensely) can all inhibit free exchange of information. Conversely, the presence of these SOLER factors will facilitate communication by fostering the listener's receptivity and conveying their presence to the speaker.

Presence as Non-Interruption

In listening to youths, ideally the message to convey should be one of attentiveness and understanding. All too often, however, it is not understanding for which one is naturally poised; rather it is the anticipation of the first opportunity to "jump in" and present an "adult" point of view. There is a readiness to correct, amend and rebut the adolescent's positions.

This tendency to prepare an answer or advice as the youth speaks creates a condition in which one can only be partly present to the youth at any one time. Unfortunately, all too often, the norm is to attend briefly as they begin their disclosure and then jump to conclusions about what they are about to say; in other words, the adult mentally backs out of the interaction to prepare a helpful response. The adolescent is not fooled, though, as the blank, distant stare which accompanies the "mentally backing out" is received by him or her as an uncaring, unconcerned attitude and thus can prove quite detrimental to the relationship.

In addition to the potential harm to the relationship, such non-presence impedes accurate understanding of the ongoing exchange. In backing out of the interaction in order to prepare a response, one fails to hear all that is said. The result is oftentimes an embarrassing display of one's own inattentiveness. For instance, when the adult mentally formulates a position (thus arriving at the apparent "undeniable truth"), he or she may find himself or herself almost impulsively interrupting the youth in mid-sentence with a "Yes, but!" response. These interruptions, and packaged rebuttals will tell the youth that this is *not* a genuine exchange and that once again, like the many others with whom he or she has tried to talk, this adult also really does not care to listen.

Facilitating Communication Through Empathetic Listening

In addition to creating their own, somewhat cryptic language, adolescents are often indirect in the expression of their feelings and their concerns. This indirectedness is based on both their desire for personal privacy and their fear of possible negative reactions from the adult listener. To deal with this, there is a need to develop the skills which facilitate reaching out and actively gathering the information which adolescents find so hard to disclose. Such reaching out involves the employment of active, empathetic listening skills, and creating an environment of trust and support.

As youths most of us have been instructed to be "quiet, polite, listeners." While such directives can be instructive in terms of reminding us not to be interruptive, or judgmental, it is quite misleading if one is to conclude that listening is a passive process. Momentary inattentiveness may quickly escape to fantasy or intrusion of one's personal concerns when there is an attempt to remain passive recipients in a communication process. In order to reduce this non-attendance, an active-empathetic stance should be assumed. Listening, when it is facilitative, is actually an active, and often exhausting process. Good listeners do not simply sit back and passively absorb and record information provided by the speaker but rather reach out and involve themselves in the data gathering process.

Active listeners need to step out from behind their perspectives and step into the phenomenal world of the speaker so as to experience the world as he or she experiences it. Seeing the world as the speaker does will facilitate the reception of his or her messages as they are fully intended. The parent or counselor confronted by a distraught adolescent may find it difficult to understand and appreciate his decision to not go to the prom, thus forfeiting the money he paid for the flowers, ticket and rental of formal wear, all because his "girl" told him that she would like to "date other guys rather than continue going steady." As adults we may frequently fail to see this somewhat extreme and costly (at least financially) decision as based upon a reaction to a serious, near catastrophic event. It may be hard to view the loss of one's "steady" as a serious problem. One may even offer some superficial comment, such as, "After all, you still can be friends and go out," or one can devalue the relationship by suggesting that he "would be a fool to waste all that money over something so ridiculous."

The intensity of the situation may, however, be more fully appreciated if efforts were taken to step into the adolescent's shoes and view it from his perspective. Consider a somewhat parallel situation for adults. One's spouse arrives home one evening and announces that after much thought he has decided to share his life with another, *in addition* to being with you. Everyone would probably agree that this qualifies as serious and that attempts to console the person experiencing it with comments such as, "Hey, but you still can be friends. After all, you don't spend all of your time together now—so what's the big deal?" would not only be unappreciated but might be seen as somewhat uncaring and callous. I am not suggesting that these situations are equal, but rather I am attempting to highlight the point that "seriousness" is often in the eye of the beholder. Consequently, if there could be an appreciation and *sense* of the desperation experienced by this youth (perhaps as great as that of the spouse in the above example), one would most certainly be more inclined to be attentive to him at this time of crisis.

In order to increase our sense of empathy for adolescents, there is a need then to begin to empty oneself and allow youths to unload their experience to someone who has the space to receive it. Shedding personal concerns and experiences, one needs to enter their world, the perspective of youths in crisis. This is not an easy task, and it requires that separation of the messages sent by youths from those that are self-generated.

In attempting to completely understand the messages being sent, it is important to not only receive and record the adolescent's communication but also to feed back to the youth for validation of its accuracy what was received and interpreted. Thus stopping the youth periodically and simply asking "Is this what you mean?" or restating what has been said in our own terms will help to ensure our active attendance and receptive accuracy.

Empathy also means entering the private world of another without making judgments. It involves placing one's understanding into words that the adolescent can understand. It entails sensing meanings of the message behind the words or in between the lines, often messages about which the adolescent is only partly aware.

In order to begin to move into the adolescents' phenomenal experience and to see their world through their angle of vision and thus begin to understand the meaning of the words as they are intended, it is necessary to develop both primary level and advanced level accurate empathy skills.

The first level of accurate empathy (that is, primary empathy) requires the listener to restate, or actively reflect to the speaker, the "explicit" message presented. This is not mere parroting of the words that the youth presents, but a reflection of the *explicit* message received. This is done in order to demonstrate to the speaker that (a) we are in attendance and truly listening and (b) that the message received is the message he or she intended. For example:

> *Adolescent:* "The dance is coming up and I really don't know who to ask *(nervously laughs)*—you know, so many possible choices!"

> *Youth minister:* "It seems difficult for you to make a choice about a date for the dance."

The intent of such reflection is not to play a game or function as a tape recorder. By attending so deeply to another's message to the point that one is able to record it and feed it back will result in a more accurate understanding of what is being conveyed. Such an understanding when reflected provides evidence of a psychological presence to the adolescent and also serves as a possible stimulus for his or her own increased personal understanding of self and the issue at hand. Thus in the same exchange, the adolescent upon hearing the reflection of the explicit message regarding the difficulty of the decision may continue by adding more data to which the helper can respond further. Then the youth minister, "listening" to both the verbal message, and the non-verbal cues (such as the intonation, inflection in voice and the nervous laughter), and "hearing" the words from the perspective of the adolescent, responds to the "implicit" message.

> *Adolescent:* "Difficult . . . *(nervously laughs)*. I guess it's not the decision that's difficult."

Youth minister: 'You know, when you say 'difficult' and kind of laugh the way you do, I sense that you are feeling uptight as if you don't think you could ask anyone to the dance or perhaps that whoever you may ask won't be interested in going?"

As can be seen then in the above illustration, the youth minister in responding to the perceived implied message is actually able to give evidence of advanced empathy. This youth minister is not attempting to mind read or to be judgmental in tentatively providing these conclusions but is attempting to "completely" understand that which is being presented. Thus, the youth minister reflected what was being presented by the adolescent in light of *how* it was said (using tone of voice, body language, etc., as cues) and *what else* had been said (i.e., what is known from this client previously). It is learning how to listen to the *tone as well as the tune* which provides the material for complete understanding.

Because of the adolescent's own inability to explicate feelings and concerns, the youth minister's ability to listen between the lines, going beyond the words, or tune itself, to the rhythm, the implication, the meaning beneath or behind, is essential. In listening to the youth one should be asking oneself questions such as: "What is he or she trying to say?" "What is the message he or she wants me to receive?" "If I were in his or her place, what would these words mean to me?"

Such advanced empathy is a powerful tool and must be employed with care. Empathy is not blind guessing or mind reading, but it develops as a natural outgrowth of "truly being with another" and "seeing the world from his or her angle of vision." When used appropriately, such advanced empathy can help to clarify the underlying concerns and feelings the adolescent has in regard to particular issues—feelings often unclear to the adolescent himself or herself.

In attempting to develop such active-empathetic listening skill or in trying to teach adolescents and/or their parents the same skills, I have found the use of the following exercise to be quite instructional.

Active Listening Exercise

The exercise requires three persons, one acting as a speaker, one as the listener and one as a referee. It can prove quite interesting if it is possible to have the parent and the adolescent choose the roles of speaker and listener, while personally serving as "referee."

Prior to the discussion one needs to have each of the players select one of the roles and stick to it. Next, a topic is selected. In this regard I have found that it is useful to choose a subject which involves some personal investment and feeling but one which is not a "hot" topic or major point of conflict:

Step 1:   The speaker begins to discuss his/her position on the topic. For step one the listener responds as he/she might typically act. The referee simply observes and notes the effectiveness of the exchange. After approximately five minutes the referee stops the discussion. The referee shares several observations, noting areas of misunderstanding, interruption, jumping to conclusions, etc. Similarly, the listener discusses how he/she felt about the exchange—was he/she bored, inattentive, etc.? Finally, the speaker relates how he/she felt about the exchange. Did the speaker feel attended to, understood, etc.?

Step 2:   The discussion is continued with one major modification. The listener must now follow a simple rule. Prior to responding to the speaker the listener must "repeat" or paraphrase, the *explicit* content of the speaker's message (i.e., primary level empathy). The referee, for his/her part, is to ensure that this rule is followed and that the discussion is not allowed to continue until the listener actively reflects the explicit message. Should the listener's perception of what was said be inaccurate, the speaker needs to correct it. The listener then must repeat the corrected version prior to responding. This procedure is to continue for five to ten minutes. Again the referee processes the experience, noting the "difficulties" the participants may have encountered while pointing out the possible benefits of such a process.

Step 3: The roles of speaker and listener should actively alternate as would be the case in normal discussion. Again, however, each time that one takes the role of speaker (shifting from the role of listener), he/she is to preface personal comments with a reflection of the explicit message of the previous speaker's position. The referee will again prevent anyone from speaking without first reflecting accurately the message just received.

While the above exercises can be both frustrating and somewhat exhausting it should help to emphasize the difficulty we all have in actively and totally attending to one another. Further it should help to highlight the value of active empathetic listening.

Facilitating Disclosure

Even when one finds oneself, as a listener, employing active, empathetic listening skills, the adolescent's willingness to disclose may prove restricted. Often restriction or inhibition of the adolescent's disclosure is stimulated by fear of risking openness and thus vulnerability with another, particularly if the other is a valued other, such as a parent.

Nagging, sarcasm, preaching, evaluating, judging, belittling, humiliating, etc., are all responses which will act as almost insurmountable barriers to free disclosure. The youth who feels that he or she will be critically judged, and perhaps humiliated as a result of the information he or she is about to share, will certainly not disclose that information. This is not to suggest that a parent or youth worker need approve or condone everything the youth says or does but that there is a need to be cautious in distinguishing our reaction to what is said or done, as opposed to the one's reaction to the youth himself or herself.

Adolescents who feel vulnerable and concerned about another's reaction to a disclosure are more apt to open up to an individual whom they feel that they can trust. It is important to provide youths with an awareness that they will not be judged, evaluated, or put down, or that the information they disclose will not be used against them.

Even when such a stage is set, youths still may find it difficult to respond because they are unclear about what it is they feel, or they feel inadequate in expressing themselves when it comes to "labeling" these feelings. I have found that asking adolescents to keep daily logs or diaries which highlight both their activities and their "personal" reflections provides both myself and those youths with a tool and material for mutual exploration. The private nature of the writing allows them the "control" and personal protection they need. It is completely up to them to choose what they will write, and whether or not they will share all, part or none of what has been written. Writing about their activities and personal reflections often assists adolescents to identify feelings which were confused prior to the writing. They sometimes see patterns of the activities or responses which may have been troublesome and they often report that the writings serve as a vehicle for their own problem solving.

Concluding Thoughts

Relating with adolescents can be both a highly frustrating and an immensely satisfying experience. It is an experience which requires effort and skill on the part of adults.

And so it is essential for adults (i.e., youth ministers, parents) to continue to develop the skills needed for open, accurate communication with the adolescent. As was previously noted, these skills once developed are not to be hoarded. Since they are essential to good communication, to the establishment and maintenance of a facilitative relationship and to true understanding, these skills should be shared with the adolescent, their teachers and their parents.

Reference

Egan, G. *You and Me.* Monterey: Brooks/Cole, 1977.

Recommended Readings

Adler, R.B., Rosenfeld, L.B. and Towne, N. *Interplay*. New York: Holt, Rinehart and Winston, 1980.

Egan, G. *You and Me*. Monterey: Brooks/Cole, 1977.

Egan, G. *The Skilled Helper*. Monterey: Brooks/Cole, 1975.

Ruffner, M. and Burgoon, M. *Interpersonal Communication*. New York: Holt, Rinehart and Winston, 1981.

Chapter 4

Moving Toward Independence and the Art of Letting Go

I can still remember the first time, holding my breath and silently saying a prayer, as I let go of the seat of my son's two wheeler. I was clearly announcing to the world his ability to ride and my ability to let go! Letting go, and being let go, in all of its varied forms (i.e., letting go of a toddler's hand, to eagerly await his or her first steps; handing over the keys of the family car for the first time to a sixteen year old, etc.) can be both an exhilarating and somewhat traumatizing experience. Fostering a child's growth toward independence and psychological emancipation is one of the most difficult yet most needed of all parenting duties.

The anxiety that parents experience when their toddler "breaks away" from parental support in order to stand alone, or when their preschooler "goes it alone" in learning to ride a bike, is minor in comparison to the possible tension experienced by the parents of an adolescent who is attempting to gain emancipation from the family. Adolescents' attempts at individuation—developing their own style, or making their own statement—can be extremely traumatizing for adolescents and parent alike.

The Push, the Pull of Psychological Weaning

Just as the fetus needs to separate from his or her mother and begin the process of individuation, constantly moving toward greater independence, so too must adolescents wean themselves from social-emotional dependency upon their families. "Breaking away"—physically, emotionally, socially—are all prerequisites to adolescents' assumption of their roles as adults of the next generation. Unlike early school age children who, while playing with their peers, "live" and operate in their parents' world, adolescents realize at some level that they will play now in a society of their peers, but that this same society will eventually replace the society of their parents. Unlike their younger brothers and sisters, adolescents do not merely play at stepping into their parents' shoes. Instead they start to become aware that it is *their own* shoes which they need to step into, since they will replace those of their parents.

The transition from child to adult requires that adolescents shed their old, child-like style. In surrendering the role of child, with all of its characteristic ways of thinking, and behaving, especially those reflecting physical, social and psychological dependency, the adolescent takes on a new style, a new stance—one which is independent socio-emotionally from family bonds.

During the early phases of this weaning process, adolescents will often go out of their way to shed the trappings of childhood. Quite often the shedding takes the form of a new haircut, new clothes, unusual language, and pronounced mannerisms which often challenge the family's traditions and values. At this time, parents may begin to question where are those "A" and "B" grades they were so accustomed to, or where is the clean-cut youth they used to call "son" or "daughter." In such instances if these same parents view the shedding of the old style as a rejection of them as parents, and as an expression of non-love, then they may wonder "Where did we go wrong?"

Confronted by the sense that their child is "breaking away," many parents may experience concern over loss of control, or the sense that their own importance has been diminished by the adolescent's new-found sense of autonomy. Such parents, feeling a sense of panic, may attempt to regain what once was by imposing tighter control and attempting to force dependency through increased rules, regulations and restrictions. However, forcing dependency and control, in the name of authority and respect, may well result in damage to the youth, the parents themselves and the adult-adolescent relationship.

Youth ministers have often been confronted by adolescents and parents in a crisis which has resulted when a minor point over independence has skyrocketed to a battle over power and control. Tommy and his father (Mr. H) were just such a case. For the first fourteen years of his life, Tommy followed in the footsteps prescribed by his father. An excellent student, clean-cut (for Tommy's father that meant a short haircut, mannerly and respectful), Tommy was, according to Mr. H, "just what a kid was supposed to be!"

The beginning of the battle lines were drawn with Tom's entrance into high school. The high school experience introduced Tom to new friends, new challenges and new opportunities to experiment with his own personal style. At first the arguments between Dad and son were minor. Minor confrontations about the music being too loud or the telephone conversations too long. But these were only the precursors of what was to come. The first report card announced the clear demarcation. Tom's grades which were primarily C's were not what Mr. H expected, nor would he accept them. Tom was grounded for the entire second marking period and restricted from "hanging out" with those other kids who were clearly "bad influences."

The grounding was not only seen as an inconvenience, a punishment (just or otherwise) by Tom, but more as a humiliating announcement to all *his* friends that Tom was still quite immature, and dependent on the "old man." The battle lines were now clearly drawn!

The issue was not simply good or bad grades but one of control. "I'll show him who is in charge. He won't get away with this!" was a battle cry which both Tom and his father would quickly announce. Tom's hair started to get longer (covering his ears). His clothes became even less traditional (more jeans, T-shirts, etc.) and his defiance started to be more open and direct (talking back). Finally, by the beginning of the third marking period of this his first year in high school, Tom had "escaped" (i.e., run away) from home twice, and he and his father had on more than one occasion come close to punches following a shouting match.

Granted, this is not the typical case, but sadly it is one with which youth ministers are well acquainted. Holding on to the point of strangulation simply will not work, and the parent and adolescent need to be assisted in knowing how to "break away," "let go," "wean" in ways which are healthy and productive for all involved.

Parents need assistance in recognizing that their youth's attempt at shedding the old and finding the new is not a reflection of their parenting going wrong but of it going right. These parents need to appreciate that God has made "everything appropriate to its time" (Eccl 3:11) and the time of adolescence is one for seeking to express individuality and independence. Granted, all too often the early attempts are a bit extreme (orange striped hair?), but parents need to begin to appreciate that overkill is in most instances a better sign than "no kill" at all.

While not every adolescent goes to such extremes of selection and expression of his or her identity, even those who appear to show little if any external sign of shedding the old self and style are in the process of sorting, evaluating, experimenting and eventually selecting a "style" which announces their own "individuality" and independence.

Independence as Goal

It has always been interesting to me (and a point often raised by many of the adolescents with whom I have contact) that the same parents who preach to their adolescents to "stand tall," and to make their own decisions instead of being mere sheep following their peers, often react negatively when their children, taking their advice, attempt to question or challenge their parents' rules and regulations. It is almost as if "independence" and "self-reliance" are OK as long as they do not interfere with parental power and control. The pride and sense of satisfaction most parents derive from observing the growing independence of their toddler is absent when confronted by the increased demand for autonomy by their adolescent. Yet, it is this same pride and sense of satisfaction which needs to return if parents are to facilitate their youth's movement toward the goal of independence.

Independence and self-sufficiency are established as personal goals for both child and parents starting at birth. Parents work hard at fostering their infant's independence in the areas of feeding, dressing, walking and self-expression. Parents, proud as can be about the new-found independence of their child, may, like Shelley's Dr. Frankenstein, wonder exactly what type of "creature" they have created, especially as the "self-assured" two year old looks squarely into their eyes and announces assertively: No!

Promoting independence is risky. Parents are often concerned that if their adolescent is encouraged to make decisions, he or she may make them differently than the way the parents would have! The adolescent may say "No" not just to the parents' request to "get down from there" or "not to touch," as was the case in childhood, but to the parents' life style, values, or perhaps even—to the parents.

Seeking independence is difficult for adolescent and parent alike. It is normal for parents to fear that harm to myself or to my child may result from my "letting go." Holding on, however, denies and delays the emancipation process and will do more harm by fostering resentment and hostility on the part of adolescent or by promoting continued dependency and emotional crippling. Surely such crippling is not, nor has it ever been, most parents' goal.

Even when independence is the parents' goal and they perceive that their child is growing up, and therefore expect him or her to act as grown-ups do, parents may out of force of habit find themselves still treating their youth as a child. For instance, it is not that unusual for parents of a thirteen year old to "unconsciously" employ a sixteen year old "baby sitter" to watch him or her for a couple of hours while the parents go out to an early show. Likewise, a parent who has for years selected the school clothes each fall may continue that practice well beyond the point it is necessary. As was noted, letting go is not easy; it requires a conscious and considerate effort on the parents' part.

Increased independence is also difficult from the adolescents' perspective. One difficulty, insofar as adolescents are concerned, is the inconsistency of the whole process. Although they feel that they have grown up and thus want to be treated that way, they may still exhibit childish habits and desires. Adolescents found protesting the injustices of government policies or confronting the perceived hypocrisy of the Church as an institution may be the same "children" who find cartoons or water balloons quite enjoyable.

God certainly has made "everything appropriate to its time" (Eccl 3:11), and for adolescents it is a time of becoming, a time of transition, a time of moving from one developmental position to another. These swings from point to point will be evident to all and confusing to most.

What Can We Do?

Clearly letting go is difficult for all involved, but let go we must! Fostering adolescent growth toward independence and psychological emancipation requires a proper blending of support, guidance and freedom to choose and select. It is a balance not easily achieved. The push-pull of the emancipation is one which causes rifts, sometimes minor, quite often major, within families. And so, youth ministers have to be prepared to help both adolescents and their parents through this transition and on to healthy interdependence.

Assisting the Adolescent

In the search for independence, and the attempt to shed the bonds of dependency, adolescents quite often err in the direction of excess. Throwing out baby *and* bathwater, adolescents may find that in their attempts to gain freedom, they in fact shackle themselves to ongoing dependency of another sort. An example of this is the adolescent who in an attempt to demonstrate total emancipation quits school, only to find a consequential increased dependency on others because of limited job skills or vocational preparation. Another illustration is the many reported cases of the "liberated" youth who runs away in the ultimate statement of emancipation, only to find himself or herself enslaved in low paying jobs, street existence, and even crime. Adolescents, while desiring independence, need assistance in gaining a sense of moderation for their expressions of independence.

Youth ministers can play a very important role in affirming adolescents in their growing sense of personal selfhood, while at the same time reinforcing the need for continued openness to future experience and input from others, such as their parents. There is a real need to assist adolescents to see that "independence" is something which comes not from saying No to everything and everyone, but from learning how to say "yes" to one's own sense of self-reliance and one's own ability to make responsible and thus consequential decisions. There is a need for them to appreciate that independence comes from making mature, consequential decisions. It is not the fact that one can stay out as late as one wants that delineates independence. Rather, mature social-emotional independence comes from the knowledge that to come in at a certain hour will result in a certain set of consequences and, upon reflection of the personal impact of such consequences, making a decision as to what is most reasonable and effective given this set of contingencies. Making reasonable and responsible decisions and value judgments are the signs of emancipation—of becoming one's own person.

Adolescents are confronted by a number of situations which demand resolution and value choices. Drugs, alcohol, and sexual activities are but a few of the more highly publicized issues requiring the adolescent to make individual choices. Adolescents need to develop the capacity to understand and assess their own values while not being shaken from them by pressure from their peers. Therefore, it is in learning to clarify their values and to employ consequential thinking that adolescents gain the personal independence being sought.

Teaching Consequential Thinking

In teaching youth to employ consequential thinking I found that a number of specific steps need to be considered. First, like most of us, adolescents may be certain as to the fact that they are unhappy or dissatisfied, while uncertain as to what specifically is the problem. A clear goal is necessary for responsible decision making, yet many adults and clearly most adolescents fail to clarify their goals *prior* to responding. *Problem identification and definition* is the first step which I attempt to teach a youth in the process of developing consequential thinking. The youth needs to be assisted in analyzing the situation clearly and defining it in specific, concrete terms. It does very little in terms of facilitating problem-solving if the adolescent uses absolute, black-and-white, evaluative terms in defining the problem. Saying "My parents are the worst" doesn't rapidly lead to a solution or a decision on how best to respond to the situation. However, by redefining the problem in concrete, behavioral terms, such as "They have a 10 o'clock curfew," "I receive only $5.00 allowance," or "They select all of the clothes that I have to wear," will begin to facilitate the process of problem solving and goal attainment.

It is not only necessary to teach adolescents to be more specific, more concrete, in their problem articulation. Also, it is necessary to help them learn to separate out the "real facts" of a situation from the personal evaluation or opinion as to the meaning of those facts. For example, the youth considering quitting school because he sees himself as a real failure and someone who will never be able to succeed needs to recognize that being a failure is not *the problem,* but an opinion and belief which perhaps resulted from the problem. Consequently, this youth needs to be encouraged to be less evaluative and more descriptive of the situation so that a redefinition of the situation from "I am a failure" to "I failed my four major subjects this year because I played around at night and didn't do *any* homework" can result. The facts of the problem (i.e., not doing any homework) can lead to more reasonable solutions (e.g., doing homework) than does the originally defined problem of being "a failure."

This point of assisting the adolescent to separate fact and opinion when defining an area of concern or a desired goal is especially important for those youths who "blindly" equate anything *new* with "good" and "desirable," and anything *old* or *out of date* with "bad" and "avoidable." The temptation to seek it, do it, use it, just because it is the latest, can obviously lead to a variety of ill-fated consequences, ranging from simply losing some money, as in the case of buying the latest gadget which shortly proves itself to be worthless, to losing one's life by experimenting with the latest and "best" drug. Therefore, helping youths separate out the facts of the situation in order to see it as it is, so they don't jump to the conclusion that it is "in" and so must be "good," will assist them in making responsible, consequential decision.

Once the problem and the subsequent goal or solution has been identified (*problem identification*), then the second step in the consequential thinking process is *path finding.* Once the desired outcome is identified, adolescents need to be assisted to articulate a number of possible alternative paths or routes to goal attainment and problem solution. In this phase techniques such as brain storming are useful. The procedure would be to use this technique with the adolescent, myself and their parents (if they are in attendance) to generate as many solutions as possible. At this early stage of path finding the solutions need not be feasible nor even desirable. The goal here is simply to create quantity of solutions. Quality will be assessed in a later stage. Often what initially appears to be a ludicrous solution may in fact turn out to be the most profitable.

As the solutions are being generated, they are written down without any verbal evaluation or criticism. During this phase, adolescents are taught that no possible solution should be excluded.

In this process open-ended questions are used to encourage youths to consider solutions which might often prove helpful. Youth ministers can introduce an idea with an open ended phrase such as "Have you thought about . . .?" or "What about . . .?" There should be an avoidance of offering suggestions by prefacing it with "You should" or "You ought" or any other comment which might suggest that the adult's approach is the best if not the *only* solution. This point is extremely important, especially when the parents are working as co-trainers. If the goal was simply to solve a problem, then perhaps it would be effective and economical for those with the most expertise and experience (for example, the parents) to provide the solution. However, helpers should remind themselves and the parents that the goal is not simply problem solving but a fostering of a sense of responsible, independent decision making within their youths. Thus it is *their* decisions, and not their acquiescence to the adult's decision, which is being sought.

The third step in the process is to evaluate the consequences of each possible alternative route to problem solving (*evaluation*). This analysis will help the youth make the best decision. Again, working along with adolescents there is a need to ask them to consider the situation in a "what if" format in an attempt to predict positive and negative consequences which may result. Consequences to employing one or another alternative may include such things as: benefits gained by them or others, problems caused for them or others, feelings that could be aroused, or the costs (emotionally, financially, physically) involved. Analyzing each alternative in this way will not only help the adolescent choose the best plan of action for any one particular problem or goal but will begin to help them to develop a "consequential" form of thinking and deciding. Learning to "think ahead" and consider all the possible ramifications of one's decision is a major step in developing the sense of responsibility which each parent seeks for his or her youth.

Once each alternative has been analyzed for consequences and the alternatives rated for satisfaction, the next step is to encourage the youth and provide support for their selection of a particular strategy for implementation.

Case Illustration. Figure 4-1 provides both a form found to be useful in applying the above process with youths in counseling, and an example of the types of responses often generated. The responses listed were developed while working with Mr. and Mrs. S and their daughter "Sam." The presenting complaint from Sam was that her parents were "horrible," "untrusting" and attempting to "ruin my social life."

As previously described, step 1 was to help Sam develop a more concrete, factual, less evaluative definition of the problem. As such she was encouraged to *describe* the conditions which led up to these feelings about her parents. After a general "complaint" period, Sam was continually directed to be more clear by describing specific examples, and the problem began to take shape (i.e., problem identification). Specifically the issue was that Sam's parents required her to be home by 10 P.M. on Friday evenings, a point of consternation to Sam since Friday was the "party" night and most kids stayed out until midnight. Prior to meeting with me the family attempted their own solution to the problem by compromising and accepting the mathematical average of 11 P.M. as curfew. However, this solution was not acceptable.

While the compromise appeared to make sense, it did so only if the problem was one of time. On further discussion regarding the nature of the problem and the desired goal it was found that time was not the issue but that, for Sam, it was "being embarrassed and feeling like a little kid" having to leave the party when everyone else could stay. Similarly, for the parents the issue was not a specific hour, but their own anxiety about Sam's safety.

Once the problem was identified as being Sam's desire to avoid peer humiliation and her parents' desire to know that she is safe, paths to goal attainment were brainstormed. With assistance the family was able to generate quite a number of possible solutions, ranging from not going out at all (thus parents would know she was safe) to staying out as late as she wanted with the parents getting therapy to reduce their anxiety. However, the solutions which seemed most feasible were: (1) come in at 11, (2) come in at 10 but have her parents' permission to "bad mouth" her parents in front of her peers and thus "save face," or (3) stay until 12 with the proviso that she call at 10:30 and be picked up by her father (even though the party was only one block away).

On considering the varied consequences it was decided that option three appeared to be the most rewarding and least costly and thus was accepted for implementation. Upon re-evaluation the family reported that not only did the solution work but that Sam, now knowing she could stay out, quite often found that she did not want to since she generally got tired by 11. On seeing their daughter make such responsible decisions the parents soon found that their own anxiety about her safety was greatly diminished.

Assisting the Parent

Parents are confronted with the task of promoting their adolescent's movement toward independence without going too far, too soon. These parents, like their adolescent, are in need of support and guidance. They need to be assisted in accepting the "healthiness" of the current expression of independence and they should be encouraged to seek ways to foster this emancipation.

Accepting their youth's movement toward independence requires that parents have a sense of security about themselves. The adolescent is entering a time of experimentation, a time of uncertainty and a time of possible failure and thus needs a home environment which is both emotionally stable and accepting. While parents may fear that their children will shed their values, as was previously noted, they cannot simply hold on and impose their values. It simply will not work.

Parents need to have a very well defined identity and value structure worked out so that they live what they believe. It is not sufficient to employ the "Do as I say, not as I do" approach. When the children see something in their parents which is integral to their life, a life which is attractive and functional, then these youths will have a basis for "valuing" the values they see.

The first step in facilitating the adolescent's movement toward

Figure 4-1: Teaching Consequential Thinking

PRESENTING COMPLAINT: (Case of "Sam")
Parents are horrible, ruining my life

REDEFINED PROBLEM
Conflict over issue of staying out beyond 10 P.M.

More specifically, the conflict is with Sam's need to "save face" while reducing her parents' anxiety over her safety.

ALTERNATIVE SOLUTIONS	POSITIVE CONSEQUENCES	NEGATIVE CONSEQUENCES
1. Come in at 11	*one hour later *parents off my back *getting parents to begin to compromise	still embarrassed, still one hour before 12.
2. Come in at 10 with permission to "bad mouth" parents	"save face" parents acceptance	still in at 10 and feel guilty
3. Stay out until 12 parents pick up	*out until 12 *parents feel she's safe	have to explain about "pick up"

DECISION

Select option 3—stay out until 12 but call at 10:30 and be picked up by father.

RE-EVALUATION

After trial period of three weeks family found this solution worked, that is, Sam was happy, parents not as anxious. In addition the trial demonstrated that Sam could be responsible as evidenced by her coming home early by 11 on those nights she was tired.

independence is for parents to develop an accepting attitude. Such an acceptance requires that parents know and understand their adolescent and the adolescent experience, as well as feel secure in themselves as people—as parents. Parents who viewed the toddler's "No's" as threats to their authority will certainly not be able to accept or affirm the adolescent's striving for independence.

As youth ministers there is a need to assist the parents to *know* and *understand* the adolescent experience and recognize the value in "seeing" their adolescent as a *person,* with unique needs, gifts and talents—and the rights and responsibilities that accompany such personhood. (See 1 Corinthians 12:4.)

Those parents who, from fear, or guilt or some other self-serving motive, attempt to tie their adolescent down need to be confronted. Youth ministers need to confront them with their own parenting goals. These parents need to articulate the hopes and aspirations they hold for their youths while at the same time assess how their "holding on" runs contrary to the attainment of these goals.

One of the difficulties one faces when attempting to encourage parents to let go is that manipulation and control through shame, guilt, and coercive power often prove temporarily effective. Parents who note this result need to be shown that such temporary effectiveness comes at a high price. The cost of such "control" is often stifled freedom and development. Youths reared under such control often demonstrate crippling dependency, exaggerated insecurity and resentment of their parents.

Parents need to demonstrate an acceptance of the adolescent as a person. The adolescent can no longer be viewed as simply an addendum to the family, or another offspring—"son" or "daughter." As youth ministers the need then is to help parents see and cherish the uniqueness which is their youth. With such an attitude these parents will be able to manifest the unconditional love essential to the youth's ongoing growth and development. Conveying to their children that, regardless of the "style" they developed or experimented with, they will always be loved for what they are, not how they look or act, is an important key to adolescent development.

Parents who are able to "see" the wisdom of this position can find support in the stance taken by the father of the prodigal son. For like him, parents need to remain loving, even though their son or daughter may break away from all that they hold dear. With such an attitude they will be ready and able to extend their open arms in unconditional love to their children upon their return to their family, announcing: "Let us eat and celebrate because this son of mine was dead and has come back to life. He was lost and is found" (Lk 15:23).

In addition to having the appropriate attitude about their adolescents and their movement toward emancipation, parents need to develop the *skills* or *parenting practices* which provide for such independence.

Parents need to promote increased independence in a gradual, step-like fashion so as to provide their adolescent with the essential balance between the stimulation of independence and the sense of security found in knowing the support of his or her family. Adolescents must be allowed as much independence as they can responsibly handle.

As one might surmise, determining what is "as much" is quite a difficult task and may require a bit of trial and error. One caution that often needs to be made with parents is that increasing one's boundaries is scary and certainly does open the child to greater possibility of failure and harm. Therefore, parents need to recognize that it is OK, in order to reduce the possibility of real harm and reduce their own anxieties, to begin with small steps. Providing youths with small opportunities for independent action and decision making is at least the first step. It is a step which when proven successful will further reduce the apprehension and anxiety the parents may feel about letting go, and thus encourage a continuance of the process. Starting out in small steps is acceptable, as long as they continue to open up and let go to a degree commensurate with the youth's demonstration of the ability to function successfully within these broader limits.

Youth ministers can facilitate the parents' "shaping" of the adolescent's opportunity for independence by helping them to establish a clear conceptualization of what they would like to eventually allow their child to do and then secondly to break this ultimate goal down into smaller, sequential subgoals or steps. For example, parents who would like to be able to leave their son or daughter home alone over a weekend while they go away need to consider allowing the youth to stay home without a sitter one evening, then to stay alone and care for himself or herself for an entire day with the parents returning later that evening, and eventually allowing the youth to spend one night alone, etc. If the parents can be assisted to establish such subgoals, then the youth's increasing ability to handle the responsibility can be tested and evaluated under "safe" conditions.

Independence does not happen overnight. Weaning is an ongoing process started at birth. Cutting the umbilical cord not only announces the separation and independence of the fetus from the womb, but serves as a precursor of the whole individuation process. Successful weaning continues through these early years and well through adolescence. And so, parents need to inculcate and promote a sense of self-sufficiency and self reliance at each stage of development.

This increasing self-sufficiency on the part of the adolescent does not simultaneously obviate a reasonable dependence upon one's parents. Rather it fosters in the youth an appreciation of the unique gifts and resources that each individual possesses and inculcates in him or her the value of the movement from dependency through independence to a sense of "interdependence."

Concluding Thoughts

Adolescence is a time of choices and decisions. It is a time of becoming. It would be easy for adults who are significant in the lives of adolescents to make choices for them. So, there is a temptation to use one's experience to decide to help adolescents avoid much of the hurt and disappointment they will experience in choosing on their own. However, although this desire seems worthy, it must be remembered that such an action may rob adolescents of the opportunity to choose, and with it the opportunity to develop mature ability to choose.

God has given adults stewardship over their children. Yet, in the truest sense they are actually his children. As Kahlil Gibran noted in *The Prophet,* our "children are not your children; they are the sons and daughters of life's longing for itself; they come through you but not from you, and though they are with you, yet they belong not to you. You may give them your love but not your thoughts, for they have their own thoughts; you may house their bodies but not their souls, for their souls dwell in the house of tomorrow which you cannot visit, not even in your dreams. You may strive to be like them but seek not to make them like you, for life goes not backward, nor tarries with yesterday."

Yes, it is scary to let go, but let go we must. Adults have both a duty and a responsibility to love, respect, and guide children and youth toward independence, freedom and responsible decision making. There is clearly a need on their part to be involved in the process of individuation, the process of discovering who they are. There is also a real need to enable them to make choices responsibly by providing them with the maximum freedom they can successfully handle, the ongoing guidance and support they need, and the ever-present state of unconditional love and acceptance they deserve.

However, once again it cannot be overemphasized that letting go is "scary." Youth ministers, therefore, have an opportunity to assist parents through the moments of anxiety and concern by helping them to trust: trust in their own previous training, trust that they have laid a foundation for reasonable decision making, trust that they have provided the opportunities needed throughout their child's development to encourage a sense of competence and self-sufficiency, trust that the values they have inculcated remain to serve as the basis from which their children will stamp their own unique identity, and, most certainly, trust in the Lord. "Though you may have been driven to the farthest corner of the world, even from there will the Lord, your God, gather you; even from there will he bring you back. The Lord your God will then bring you into the land which your fathers once occupied, that you may occupy it, and he will make you more prosperous and numerous than your fathers" (Deut 30:4–5).

With such knowledge parents may then trust, amidst the turmoil, that like the prodigal son who said, "I will break away and return to my father, and say to him, "Father, I have sinned against God and against you; I no longer deserve to be called your son" (Lk 15:18), so too will their children, who are breaking away, return.

Recommended Sources for Additional Information

Auer, J. *Sorting It Out with God.* Liguori, Missouri: Liguori Pub., 1985.

Booraem, C., Flowers, J. and Schwartz, B. *Help Your Children To Be Self-Confident.* Englewood Cliffs: Prentice-Hall, 1978.

Ellis, A., Wolfe, J.L. and Moseley, S. *How To Raise an Emotionally Healthy and Happy Child.* New York: Institute for Rational Emotive Therapy, 1980.

McCoy, K. *The Teenage Survival Guide.* New York: Simon & Schuster, 1981.

Audio visual training program for youth workers, parents and youth of the various issues confronting adolescents can be obtained through:

Sunburst Communications:
39 Washington Avenue
Pleasantville, N.Y. 10570–9971

Chapter 5

Sex and the Adolescent:
An Issue Broader Than Birds and Bees

My brother recently called to wish me a happy birthday and my oldest son answered the phone. Halfway through my brother's version of "Happy Birthday," he realized that it was my son and not I who was the recipient of his fine rendition. "Kristian, you sound just like your Dad!"

At the age of thirteen my son not only is sounding like me, but he is looking like me. The deeper voice, the larger feet and the use of my razor on his yet developing beard are all public announcements of my son's entry into sexual maturity.

"Sexual maturity" are two words which often create a noticeable degree of anxiety among parents of adolescents. Comments such as "I guess I'll have to talk with him" or "I don't know what to say, or how to say it!" reflect this uncertainty and discomfort as parents contemplate having their "father-son" or "mother-daughter" talks.

Adolescence is, by definition, that period of development initiated with the growth of primary and secondary sex characteristics. Puberty is the beginning of sexual maturity but it is *not* also the beginning of sexuality. While announcing that the youth is now capable of fathering/mothering offspring, puberty is certainly not the beginning, or the ending for that matter, of one's sexual development. Sexual development involves knowledge of one's body and biological drives along with the developing sense of one's gender identity and the accompanying social-sex roles. Sexual development starts at birth and will continue through life.

Adolescence is but "another," albeit significant, time at which sexual identity and sexuality will be re-examined. It is a time involving more than simply the growth of the adolescent's sex organs, or the stimulation and arousal of sex hormones and the drive toward intimacy. It entails a reassessment of sexual identity, sex roles and sexual orientation. For youths and their parents, the adolescent's sexual awakening is often an event which is accompanied by much confusion, concern and anxiety, and a period which demands a number of personal, value-based decisions. It is an event through which both adolescents and their parents are often in need of support and guidance.

A Crisis . . . A Catastrophe

Tom and Rita were quite obviously upset. I asked Tom to explain what had transpired between them and their seventeen year old son Mark to bring them to this point of upset. Tom took my inquiry as an invitation to begin to berate his son, calling him a "pervert" and "an immoral degenerate." Intercepting the conversation, I pointed out that I was unclear about what was going on and that rather than labeling or name calling it would help me instead if they could describe what had happened to produce their concern and elicit this reaction.

It was clear that one of the immediate tasks I was faced with was to defuse some of the anger being manifested by the family members. As the discussion continued I found that Rita had arrived home, unexpectedly, that afternoon, and found her son and his girlfriend on the couch (he on top of her), fully clothed but quite obviously involved in heavy petting. The discovery of their son's emerging sexual interest acted as a cinder for the resultant fire which found its way into my office. Mark's entry into adolescence appeared to bring with it not only his own sexual awakening, but the awakening and arousal of his parents' own anxieties about sex and their role as parents as well.

Many parents are brought into the awareness of their adolescent's emerging sexual development through similar "discoveries" of their child engaged in sexual activity, by finding a pornographic magazine, by discovering a contraceptive device in their child's room, or by simply discovering the effects of sexual activity (be it a "hickey" or a pregnancy). For many parents such an introduction is received and responded to as if it were an absolute catastrophe—an event of crisis proportions.

While not trying to minimize the impact of such a discovery, the reality is that adolescents are, will be, and should be sexually awak-ened. It is not a crisis or a catastrophe but a "gift" as is indicated in the following psalm.

"You made all the delicate, inner parts of my body, and knit them together in my mother's womb. Thank you for making me so wonderfully complex! It is amazing to think about. Your workmanship is marvelous and how well I know it" (Ps 139:13–16).

One's sexuality is a special gift of life in that it requires particular understanding and responsible decision making. In light of this, youth ministers are called to assist both parents and adolescents to understand the "beauty" and "mystery" of this gift of sexuality, and to assist youths in developing the knowledge and strength required to respond to this gift in a way which will facilitate their own personal and spiritual growth.

While each single event announcing the sexual maturity of an adolescent need not be a crisis, the unbridled, and most often ill-informed, response of parent and youth to this maturity can certainly take on crisis proportions. Adolescent pregnancy, abortions and ve-neral diseases are, and have been, on the incline. A major problem, though, is the "sexploitation" of the youth market.

For fun and especially profit, sex is presented on movie screens, records, videos and television. One only need watch TV commercials advertising jeans, perfume, etc., to recognize that the focus on sexual attractiveness and stimulation is the primary marketing strategy. With such sexploitation via the mass media, one can expect an in-crease in both sexual interest and activity among those so exploited. It is not surprising, then, that in a study spanning some twenty-five years, Strommen and Strommen (1985) noted that among the eight thousand adolescents surveyed there was a significant drop in the number who viewed premarital intercourse as wrong.

Quite often parents point to such statistics and note that kids today "know too much" and what is needed is less talk about sex. Contrary to this position, if there is one thing to be learned from these statistics it is that adolescents know enough to get them into trouble but may not know enough to make the appropriate decisions to prevent it or get themselves out. Most adolescents are actually anxious and ill-informed about sexuality and appropriate sexual values. For instance, I have worked with adolescents who are convinced that "if you really love your partner, God will not punish you by giving you V.D." or that "if you stand while having intercourse you won't become pregnant," or that, as one recent client informed me, if you drink a specific diet soda prior to having intercourse, you cannot become pregnant. Such misinformation about the biological workings of the body is not unusual and clearly opens youths to the possibility of a number of serious consequences. In addition to such misinformation about the physiological aspects of their emerging sexuality, most adolescents are also unclear about the psycho-social aspects of sexuality and the importance of their own development of a value-based decision making orientation to sexual expression. Most adolescents wish they could discuss the sexual dimension of their life with their parents or some other significant adult. Yet, it is an area shrouded in myth, mystery, fear, and confusion, and it is an aspect of their life which often places them in both legal and moral dilemmas. If there is a crisis, then it is one of limited communication between parent and child or in the education of the adolescent to the various important and beautiful aspects of human sexuality. What is needed is not prohibition and restriction of information, but guidance and support.

While the primary role of educator falls to the parent, others are often called upon because of their expertise or position to assist in the education and counsel of the adolescent. Included in this group are certainly those in Christian leadership/helping roles who interact with youths (i.e., those whom I am broadly referring to here as "youth ministers"). Youth ministers should capitalize on the unique position and opportunity they have to foster the understanding of the dilemmas accompanying the sexual awakening of adolescence. Thus both parents and youths will be better prepared to make the wise, value-based decisions that are required of this period.

Wisdom and Counsel for the Adolescent

Sexual maturation involves the adolescents' growing understanding of their own sexual drives, interests, and values, as well as the acceptance of the responsibility for their sexual self and the response being made to their own sexuality. It is a developmental challenge of both sexual and spiritual proportions. Adolescents are in need of wisdom and counsel to enable them to grow in these various physical and psycho-emotional changes so as to more completely respond to Christ's call: "Come, follow me."

The almost "daily" changes in their body, the urges and drives they experience, and the decisions with which they are confronted are quite disconcerting and confusing to adolescents. So, it is not surprising that when given the opportunity to ask questions or to discuss the changes which they are experiencing, many adolescents will jump at the chance.

Many teenagers, who feel unable or unwilling to discuss these feelings and concerns with their parents, would under the cover of anonymity often turn in questions to their biology or religion teacher. Teenagers want, and need, answers and direction, and youth ministers can and should respond to their need for answers. It is essential, though, that in providing the wisdom and counsel for these adolescents, youth ministers be prepared to provide accurate, honest information regarding body functioning—the process, pleasure, risks and responsibilities involved in various forms of sexual activity including answers to the special concerns regarding rape, incest, venereal disease and homosexuality.

When questions such as "Is masturbation normal?" "Do I have homosexual tendencies?" "How can I avoid pregnancy?" "Do I have V.D.?" "Is intercourse painful?" "How come I get these uncontrollable and unexplained erections?" "What is a wet dream?" go unanswered by someone with accurate, value-based information, then the youth will turn to other sources of information, be they peers, trial-and-error learning or pornographic literature. The result of such "street learning" is misinformation and often misfortune for the youth who is so educated. So, coming to grips with one's own familiarity and comfort with sexuality will help in being responsive to the needs of those adolescents seeking counsel.

Youth ministers need to honestly assess their own degree of knowledge about sexuality. They need to be able to clearly identify how personal attitudes and values may affect their interactions with this or that youth. All involved in the counseling of youth need to consider their own limits of expertise, both in terms of their knowledge of biological functioning as well as theological positions. In addition, recognizing and accepting personal biases regarding certain sexual issues and to be aware of how such biases may color the interaction with this or that youth is helpful and important. Finally, clarifying the specific goals and objectives one wishes to achieve through discussions regarding sexuality with the adolescent is also essential.

Providing Information

Quite often the anxiety experienced by adolescents regarding their sexual development rests in their equating genital size and sexual proclivity with acceptability and self-worth. Many adolescents compare themselves to the fantasized sexual ideals portrayed via the mass media or pornographic literature. As a result they are often quite anxious about the size of their genitals ("Is my penis too small?" "Are my breasts too small?") or concerned about their ineptness as a sexual partner ("Am I weird for still being a virgin?" "I don't know how to French kiss"). While a number of these questions may elicit anxiety in the adults to whom they are posed, the youths so inquiring are in need of adequate, accurate information. Asserting that they have "no right" thinking about such things, or that when the time is right they will know the answer, does little to satisfy their need for knowledge, and clearly adds to, rather than reduces, the anxiety and insecurity they feel surrounding their emerging sexuality.

Providing Clarity

Sex education, however, is more than simply facts and figures. It is essential that the adolescent begin to understand the emotions, values and responsibilities which accompany such facts and figures.

Adolescents entering into sexual maturity need counsel which will help them to make the appropriate decisions that will lead them to a fuller appreciation of the *gift* of sexuality with which the Creator has endowed them. They are in need of a clear sense and vision of Christian sexuality and its implications for mature and appropriate conditions of intimacy.

One useful technique in counseling youths who are faced with the dilemma of engaging in premarital intercourse is to have them contrast their "loving relationship" with that modeled by Christ. With Jesus as a model of intimacy the youth can begin to question whether this or that relationship is an open friendship (Jn 14:14), whether it reflects a faithfulness to self and to others (Jn 14:18), and if it reflects an appropriate willingness for self-sacrifice (Jn 15:13). This last point is frequently a cue for some extensive discussion with the adolescent. Often the youth will note that if I love him or her, then I will do what this person wants (e.g., make love). In such an instance, it is not that difficult to refocus the perception in order to uncover the point that the converse is also true (i.e., if someone loves you, then that person won't want you to do something which would make you feel bad). Furthermore, the discussion may also reveal that the youth's so-called "willingness to do for the other" is really a reflection of his or her self-centered fear of rejection or disapproval. Under such circumstances, having the youth question the possibility that the relationship is less than *mutual* and that the push toward sexual intimacy is often driven by self-centeredness can stimulate mature, responsible, value-based decision making.

In essence, then, in attempting to facilitate the youth's attempts at mature, value-based decision making, the youth minister needs to help the youth clarify underlying motives and intentions for engaging in various sexual activities. While it is clear that the adolescent, as Aristotle noted some twenty-five hundred years ago, can be a slave to passion, not all sexual activity is an action of passion. In making value-based decisions regarding their actions, adolescents need to understand the various motives lying beneath their action and we should provide them with alternative strategies for satisfying those varied drives.

Often what first appears to be unbridled passion and sexual flirtation may in fact be something much less intense. For example, the scantily clad sixteen year old female may be less involved with her sexuality than with her "inness."

A Drive for Acceptance. While the sexual impulse is strong in the adolescent it is not the only, nor necessarily the primary motivator. Adolescents are primarily concerned with acceptance and belonging. Quite often sexual behavior is a way and means to what they believe to be belongingness and intimacy.

Those engaging in sexual activity as a tool for acceptance and belonging need to be helped to feel self-respect and self-esteem so that they can come to value themselves as people and not mere sexual items. Nancy was just such a case. She had a long standing history of promiscuity, starting at the age of twelve when I first met her. Through our discussion it became quite clear that Nancy not only had an extremely negative view of herself, but truly lacked a number of important social skills which made it nearly impossible for her to fit in and become accepted.

Feeling isolated and totally alone, Nancy "discovered" that by providing sexual favors for the boys in her neighborhood, she could feel accepted and loved for at least short periods of time. The consequences of this form of gaining acceptance were not only physically and emotionally costly (having had two abortions, and being labeled) but, in fact, failed to satisfy her real need to belong. Once it was possible to see past the actions to the underlying motivation, alternative strategies for need satisfaction were developed. Social skills and assertiveness training, along with a program of dieting, provided Nancy with the needed skills and qualities to gain acceptance. In addition to such skills training, Nancy began to attend the parish CYO meetings and dances and soon found she was being accepted for who she was, and not simply for what she could/would do (i.e., provide sex).

A Drive for Intimacy. Adolescents who feel accepted by their peers may mistakenly equate sexual activity with psycho-emotional intimacy. Such youths are similarly in need of insight, of clarity. They need help to expand their definition of intimacy beyond sexual/genital involvement. Teaching, through the example of Christ, the importance of care, warmth and sharing as expressions of intimacy and providing youths with the opportunity to develop these abilities, by way of youth groups, retreats, etc., can help them to satisfy their need for intimacy without relying solely on sexual activity. The experience with Nancy and others like her has affirmed my own feelings that the role of the Church must be expanded to provide youth with the opportunity to experience "community."

A Drive for Pleasure. A number of youths recognize the motives underlying their sexual activity to be purely self-serving and hedonistic. Such youths need to be confronted with their self-absorbed, self-indulging orientation and assisted in developing a broader, more spiritually mature position on sexuality. In such instances, youth ministers need to affirm the beauty and wonderfulness of this "gift of sexuality" and assist them in developing a deeper understanding and a more wholesome acceptance of their sexual self.

Sexuality is more than the possession of certain genitalia. Sexuality involves both the self, but more specifically the self in relationship to others. Thus the constant involvement in self-indulging sexual practices is contrary to the mature expression of one's sexuality. Further, adolescents who are driven by their strong hedonistic urges need to be helped to "see" that sexuality is fully realized and made meaningful in the sacramental commitment of marriage. Sexuality represents total self-giving in a covenant relationship.

Often when youths redefine sexuality to include its interpersonal element, its function as an expression of psycho-emotional intimacy and its sacramental nature, it helps even those youths who are struggling to resist their strong drives for pleasure. Al is a good case in point. As a seventeen year old, he was very concerned with the evilness of himself and his actions since he found it hard to restrain from masturbation. All attempts at teaching Al self-restraint techniques such as relaxation strategies, cognitive reorientation and focusing techniques failed to help, since Al felt himself "doomed to be a sinner."

Through our discussions Al began to find strength in the fact of his humanity, knowing that even the apostles had times when their spirit was willing yet their flesh was weak. Accepting the difficulty which we all face in foregoing certain forbidden fruits and being aware of the need to seek assistance in our struggles helped Al to remain hopeful even when he fell short of his ideal. From this position of renewed hope Al became much more interested and eager to learn and to employ some of the previously discussed techniques for impulse control.

It is important to affirm the adolescents in their struggle. It is also important to provide youths with techniques and strategies aimed at helping them in their battle. Given the weakness of the flesh, and the constant "temptation" from the sexual stimulation found all about the adolescent's world, strategies and techniques for avoiding these temptations and redirecting these urges are important. In this specific case, reaffirming Al's humanity, while encouraging his desire to respond to Christ's call, "Come, follow me," provided the value basis from which to begin to teach Al the psychological strategies and techniques for reducing what had become a compulsive habit. The use of thought stopping techniques, and directed muscle activity, such as lifting weights, running, exercising, etc., began to prove effective in helping Al achieve his goal of control over his sexual urges.

Wisdom and Counsel for the Parents

Parents need to be informed about the nature of the adolescent's sexual development and the role and influence they, as parents, need to play in their child's sexual education.

Sexual education has for all too long been a simple matter of "don't." The role of the parent in this "education" has been one of enforcer of the "don'ts" and preventer of sexual activity. Various approaches have been used by parents or parent substitutes to prevent sexual activity among their adolescents—approaches ranging from the use of the archaic chastity belt, and its modern equivalent, the overprotective, ever-present parent as escort, through the more elaborate systems of monetary incentive for abstinence. One state lawmaker, for example, proposed legislation which would pay girls $200 on each birthday that they were not pregnant and a $2,000 bonus if they reached their eighteenth birthday without ever being pregnant.

While most parents do not resort to such extreme measures, control and prevention through the inculcation of fear ("You will be damned") and guilt ("How could you do this to me?") have often proven to be the primary methods of "sex education" implemented by parents. The idea of threat through "fear of sin" not only has a long history, but for many individuals a lasting and damaging history.

The general consensus is that such "preventive" methods are ineffective. Further, most research clearly demonstrates that such control often results in an elevated desire for the "forbidden fruit" and the increase of a number of other negative consequences, such as increased adolescent rebellion and a lowering of the adolescent's self-esteem.

Adolescent sexual behavior is inextricably linked to the dynamics of the family and the youths' perception of how the parents treat them. Chilman (1983) identified a number of factors in the life of the adolescent which break down good resolves, making sexual activity not only desired but inevitable. He noted that in addition to such factors as peer pressure, permissive social norms and friends who are sexually active, low levels of religiousness, strained parent-child relationships and minimal parent-child communications are chief among the factors associated with extra-marital intercourse. Similarly, Strommen and Strommen (1985) noted that responsible attitudes toward sexuality were associated with families who were characterized as nurturant, warm and cohesive and in which religion was manifested as an important aspect of personal and family life.

Parents need to be encouraged to remain available and willing to share information and values about sex and sexuality with their youths. Parents who are able to provide support and love rather than condemnation will prove more effective in helping their offspring to develop the appropriate attitude toward themselves and the respect for themselves and others that self-indulging sexual practices undermine.

In developing the cohesive quality and the parent-child communication network, parents also need to begin to feel comfortable with their own sexuality so that they can model responsible sexual behavior and attitudes for their adolescents. They need to demonstrate the connection between sex and love through appropriate displays of affection. Further, parents need to demonstrate that sexual contact is only one form of intimacy, along with caring for another and sharing psycho-emotionally. Such modeling by the parents will help their adolescents to gain a sense of reverence and respect for the gift of sexuality while at the same time encouraging them to seek alternative means for achieving intimacy, such as "caring" and "sharing."

One way of helping parents arrive at a comfortable and facilitative approach to the communication of sexual information and values is through assisting them to clarify their own feelings and misconceptions about sex. Often parents avoid discussing sexual issues with their adolescent for fear of saying something wrong or demonstrating their ignorance and thus revealing their own "hang-ups." These parents are in need of accurate, authoritative information regarding the physiological components of their adolescent's sexual development as well as the moral/spiritual implications of these varied changes. Youth ministers may serve as a valuable resource to adults in need of such wisdom and counsel by openly and honestly discussing the parents' concerns and by providing them with some of the very good reference material available on these topics. (A listing of such materials and references can be found at the end of this chapter.)

In addition to gaining some knowledge about the facts, parents need to be helped to recognize that what they say doesn't have to be perfect; rather, it is more important that the information be honest and accurate and presented in the form of a dialogue rather than a lecture. Most parents fear the worst when in fact the worst probably doesn't materialize. They may be surprised by the information that they already do have to share and the value of this information for their youths. Even if parents do not know the difference between the *vas deferens* and *vas efferens* or the exact function of the fallopian tubes, the fact that they are willing to discuss what they do know, and be willing to seek advice for what they don't, will prove helpful to youths in the development of their own approach to their sexual education.

For parents to avoid discussing sex with a son or daughter because it makes them feel uncomfortable is not helpful. While it is desirable to be both informed and relaxed when talking to their adolescent, parents need not feel that they have to be experts or totally at ease. It is O.K. to feel uncomfortable. It is even O.K. to be upset, or somewhat frightened and anxious. But it is not O.K. to allow these feelings to be the excuse preventing any attempts at discussion.

Much of the discomfort experienced can be diffused when the parents are helped to identify their own areas of sensitivity and anxiety and are assisted in accepting their uneasiness. Once their acceptance of uneasiness is in place it is easier to assist them in gathering the information and practice they need to reduce this uneasiness. One useful technique in this regard is to employ "role playing." The opportunity to have the helper or youth minister pretend to be their adolescent, in order "to practice" or role play the discussion they wish to have, can diffuse some of their debilitating anxiety, while at the same time giving the helper the opportunity to provide suggestions and feedback on strategies or techniques which may facilitate the process.

Most parents approach the discussion of sexuality as if it were a one time, one shot, discussion which must occur at the "right time." Further, these parents will often use the excuse that the time is not right for that special "man-to-man" or "woman-to-woman" conversation. The time to discuss sexuality is any time children or youths ask.

Parents need to be helped to learn to hear the youth's questions as they are intended and to answer them directly and as honestly as they can. It doesn't matter if the child fully comprehends the answer. What is important is that the parents are responsive and begin to develop a bond of communication with the child. Under these conditions, that which is still unanswered or unclear will be asked again.

Just as it is important for parents to begin to realize that their children *do* want to know about sexual matters, they need further to be helped to stop jumping to the conclusion that the children in fact want to know more than they are actually asking. Most of us have laughed at the story of the man who when confronted by his four year old's question "Where did I come from?" went into panic, saying, "It's too soon for this discussion, I'm not prepared," only to find out later that the child wanted to know if it was Cleveland or Columbus. Learning to hear past one's own anxieties helps to center on the youth's actual concern. One technique which parents can be taught is to reflect the question back to their child, asking, "What do you think the answer is?" The answer that the youth provides will help clarify his or her real intent and interest in asking the question. Thus, in the above situation, if the father had asked the four year old "Where do you think you came from?" he might have found out whether it was a question of locale ("I don't know; Tommy came from Houston") or physiology ("Mommy's belly button?") or even spirituality ("Heaven?"), and thus be better prepared to provide the wisdom and counsel required.

Being responsive requires that parents not only learn to listen

Adolescents in Turmoil

to their adolescent's questions but also provide an atmosphere in which questions can be asked. The adolescent in crisis, who approaches his or her parents for support, needs to hear the message, "I'm glad you came to me," regardless of how difficult the question may be for the parent to receive.

Concluding Thoughts

Sexual awakening is both a wonderful and yet concerning event. Adolescents confronting their own sexual development are in need of wisdom and counsel. Therefore, steps need to be taken to provide them with such counsel while simultaneously assisting their parents to take up the challenge of this particular period of the parenting experience.

Adolescents want to hear how adults have worked out their own answers to the varied concerns and questions which vex them. Learning to hear adolescents' questions, and responding to their questions in an honest and genuine way will provide the foundations from which they will develop their own sense of sexuality and sexual responsibility.

In Genesis the message is that the human creation is set apart from all others for it is especially made in the image of God. Knowing that we, in all our sexuality, are made in that image raises the human experience and human sexuality to the highest plane. It is this awareness and this orientation which we need to convey and share with our youth.

References

Chilman, C.S. "Coital Behaviors of Adolescents in the United States: A Summary of Research and Implications for Further Studies." Paper presented at the annual convention of the American Psychological Association, 1983.

Strommen, M.P. and Strommen, A.I. *Five Cries of Parents*. San Francisco: Harper and Row, 1985.

Shelton, C.M. *Adolescent Spirituality*. Chicago: Loyola University Press, 1983.

Recommended Materials

American Medical Association and National Education Association, pamphlets on sex education, available through American Medical Association, 535 North Dearborn Street, Chicago, Ill. 60610

Public Affairs Pamphlets, available through The Public Affairs Committee, Inc., 381 Park Ave. South, New York, N.Y. 10016

Sunburst Communication, *OK To Say No: The Case for Waiting* (Video), Sunburst Communication, Dept AW, 39 Washington Ave., Pleasantville, N.Y. 10570

Williams, Dorothy, *There Is a Season* (Video-Assisted Educational Program), Search Institute, 122 West Franklin Ave., Suite 525, Minneapolis, Minn. 55404

Chapter 6

Drugs: Use—Abuse

As the director of a large, inner city high school's guidance department, I became accustomed to late night calls from students and parents alike. One incident which still rings quite clear in my mind was that involving an eleventh grade student named Alex.

I received a call from Alex late on a Friday night asking me if I would come down to the police station to get him. It appeared that Alex had been arrested for being drunk and disorderly, and when the police arrested Alex they discovered that he was carrying three marijuana cigarettes. Alex was extremely upset and pleaded for me to come down for him. On arrival I found that the reason Alex wanted me to be with him was not so much to help him get out of the jail, but to "prevent (his) father from killing (him)."

Alex's parents arrived with his mother sobbing and pleading "What did we do wrong?" and his father blustering to all in the room, "Where is that little druggie—damm kid . . . I'll teach him!"

While the names and the setting may vary, the "story" is replayed in many police stations, homes, rectories, church halls and schools. Drug use has become quite commonplace within our culture and abuse has reached epidemic proportions.

We live in a culture where our "models" and "stars," be they from film, TV, athletics, music, or even politics, openly discuss drugs and their own drug involvement. Even "good kids" are bombarded by the message that "drinking is cool," "getting high is O.K.," and that popping this or that pill is a way to face their days. The parents of these same children, while vocally pronouncing their disdain for drug use, may manifest the culture's double standards as they laughingly proclaim that they can't function until they have their morning coffee and cigarette, or "must" have their evening cocktail in order to relax and maybe even "pop" that prescribed tranquilizer or sleeping pill to remove the stress of their extremely harried days.

Today's youth and their parents need more than drug information and police enforcement of drug laws to help them in their personal battles. They need a value basis from which to discern and make healthy, responsible decisions. It is in facilitating this discernment that youth ministers may offer an invaluable service. Youth ministers most likely have or will have contact with a child identified as using drugs and with parents who are almost frantic with concern over the possibility of their child being a "druggie." The ending to their "stories," be it tragedy or triumph, may be influenced by the response and intervention they received. This is not to suggest that people in youth ministry need to be skilled drug counselors. What is being suggested though is that anyone ministering to the needs of youth today must become more versed in some of the "whats" and "whys" of drug use so that they can help adolescents and their parents to develop and reinforce values which would conflict with drug utilization. In addition, they must help all involved to employ decision-making skills which will assist them to find creative alternatives to the "excitement," "escape," "support" and "entertainment" provided by the abuse of drugs.

The Need for Discernment

Parents, teachers, and others involved with ministering to youth often fail in their response to them when they are in need. Those involved often fail to react at all or over-react to the child using drugs. The ineffectiveness of responses like these is often rooted in their own inability to separate the user from the abuser, or the child trying to be "in" from the one "in" trouble.

Such failures in providing an appropriate response to children involved in drug use may take a number of forms. The parent noting "Thank God it's only alcohol" needs to recognize the damaging and dangerous effects of alcohol on the adolescent and the widespread nature of alcoholism among teens today. Similarly, the teacher or parent who reacts to a youth caught smoking a "joint" of marijuana by contending that he or she is addicted and in need of a detoxification program fails to discriminate between use and abuse. In both instances, there is a need for additional information regarding the *what* and *the why* of drug use among teens in order to be effective in serving them.

The informed and informing youth minister will need to discern a number of factors including the duration and frequency of the youth's involvement with drugs, the type or types of drugs being used and the apparent short and long term effects that are being evidenced. Clearly youths who have a long-standing history of drug use and exhibit drug dependency—either physical addiction (as evidenced by increased frequency and amount of drug use and signs of withdrawal) or psychological dependency (being obsessed with drug use)—must be treated differently than youths who have experimented once or twice with marijuana. Discriminating between use and abuse, between types of drugs and their impact, and determining intervention strategies based on such a discrimination is essential to begin to successfully meet the challenges being faced in light of the increased acceptance of drugs in our culture. Knowledgeable and skillful youth ministers, who can discern the varied "what's" and "why's" of each particular incident of drug use, will be able to facilitate the process of moving a parent out of crisis and a child into growth.

Discerning the What

Adolescence, as a period of development, has a long-standing history of "normative" experimentation with tobacco and alcohol. Everyone can probably reflect on one's own adolescent experiences of sneaking a cigarette behind the house, or hastily drinking a beer or whiskey at a relative's wedding or at a parent's party. While most parents will admit to the above, they find the current generation's interest in marijuana, amphetamines, and barbiturates totally incomprehensible and pathological. The casual use of soft (that is, less severely harmful or addictive) drugs is somewhat unique to this last half of the twentieth century. Yet, today it is so widespread that it can no longer be viewed as the single indicator of a youth's drug problem, or as a major pathology. As startling as it may sound, use of these drugs is in many cases simply another form of "accepted" experimentation.

Unlike their parents or grandparents, children in junior high or high school will encounter the use of marijuana, "uppers," "downers" and a variety of hallucinogenic drugs as well as alcohol among their fellow students. Whether by the example or subtle prodding of their peers, each of these youths will at some point have to make a decision to try or not to try a drug.

One group of researchers at the University of Michigan found that seven out of every ten seniors questioned from over 130 high schools in all parts of the country reported some form of illicit drug use. Similarly the National Institute on Drug Abuse found that out of a population of about 23.5 million young people between the ages of twelve and seventeen, 1.6 million have tried hallucinogens, 2.3 million have tried sniffing glue or other inhalants, 900,000 have used "angel dust" (Phencyclidine or PCP) and the number smoking cigarettes and drinking alcohol approaches ninety-five percent. Thus the social pressures facing the youths of today to use drugs and the resultant need to work with them is high. When confronted with adolescents using drugs there is a clear need to be able to help both parents and youths to discern use from abuse, as well as to discriminate which intervention strategy will prove to be most effective.

Tobacco, alcohol, and marijuana appear to be the drugs of "choice" among most youth, while other less familiar yet extremely harmful drugs such as "angel dust," heroin, cocaine, amphetamines, barbiturates and a variety of hallucinogens (LSD, THC) similarly find their way into our schools and our youth. The availability and prevalence of the "attitude of acceptability" makes discernment an essential quality for parents and youths alike. Such discernment requires a knowledge base regarding the various types of drugs currently popular along with their known short and long term effects. Such knowledge is also essential for the informed youth minister.

Table 6-1 provides a brief description of the more common street drugs along with their street names and potential effects. It should be noted that this listing is quite abbreviated. As such you are encouraged to acquire the latest information regarding the use, abuse and long term effects of drugs by contacting one of the information sources listed at the end of this chapter. Accurate, up-to-date information is essential for discernment, and the youth minister may be a primary source of such information both for the youths faced with these important decisions and for their parents.

Table 6–1: The Drugs

Marijuana (grass, pot, weed, tea, Mary Jane, rope, jays, sticks, reefer): *Cannabis sativa*, the hemp plant, contains in its leaves, flowering tops and resin the chemical THC (delta-9 tetrahydrocannabinol). THC is a psychoactive ingredient which when ingested or inhaled in low dosage tends to induce restlessness and an increased sense of well-being. Changes in the sensory perception, such as more vivid sense of sight, smell, touch, taste and hearing, may be accompanied by subtle alterations in thought formation and expression. Often the individual experiences a dreamy state of relaxation and perhaps an increased craving for sweets.

While the ill effects of short term, low dosage use are neither clear nor generally agreed upon, most researchers and clinicians will warn of the subsequent secondary dangers (for example, in driving a car) which occur as a result of the slower reaction time, distorted perception and unrealistic feelings of well-being. Research on long term, chronic users have reported lung damage, a depressing of their immune systems, the same system that fights infections, an altering of the balance of their sex hormones and possible long term memory loss.

Angel Dust (PCP, hogs, peace pills, wack, shermans): Phencyclidine (PCP) was originally developed for use as an anesthetic for animals. It is currently sold on the street in crystal, tablet or pill form or mixed with other substances in powder form. Low dosage leads to a floating, euphoric high. Higher dosages can lead to hyperexcitability, confusion, muscle rigidity, loss of concentration and memory, delirium, convulsions, violent behavior and even psychotic type reactions.

LSD (acid): A derivative from the wheat and rye fungus ergot, d-lysergic acid diethylamide, now can be made synthetically. Not physically addicting, this colorless, odorless chemical can be taken in pill or tablet form or a drop can be added to other materials (e.g., sugar cube, or cracker). Small dosages can cause changes in sensations: in vision, depth perception, color perception, time sense, hearing, etc. Sensory mixing (such as hearing color and seeing sound) can occur. Most research has demonstrated that the effects, while unpredictable, depend very much on the personality of the user and conditions (both physiological and sociological) during use. At higher dosages, hallucinations and delusions are evidenced and the user may report having religious or transcendent experiences. The facts regarding side-effects of LSD are somewhat inconsistent. Trips may produce uncontrolled panic attacks and rampant paranoia ("a bad trip"). Flashbacks (recurrence of the experience days or months later), especially if unexpected, may create additional panic and fear of insanity. Long term effects may include major mental breakdowns in an individual already emotionally unstable, or recurring anxiety and depression.

Amphetamines (speed, bennies, greenies, pilots, black beauties, footballs, cartwheels): Amphetamines are stimulants that excite the central nervous system. A high dose produces extreme feelings of euphoria and pleasure. Taken in either liquid or pill form some users dissolve the chemical for injection into the bloodstream. Even small and infrequent doses can produce destructive side-effects. Restlessness, anxiety, panic, paranoid ideation and physical exhaustion can result. Tolerance for this class of drugs is rapid (meaning that more drug will be required for the same experience), and therefore increased resources go into the acquisition of the drug and dependency results. Long term use may result in amphetamine psychosis, in which the user appears agitated, confused and paranoid. Also, injected overdoses have resulted in death.

Sedatives (downers, barbs, reds, goof balls, ludes, yellow jackets, red devils): Many drugs depress the activities of the central nervous system and are thus considered sedatives. This would include sleeping pills, tranquilizers and the class of drugs known as barbiturates. In normal prescribed doses, the sedatives depress nerve action and slow muscle reactions, including that of the heart. Heart rate and respiratory rate are slowed and blood pressure is lowered. In extreme doses, confusion, slurred speech, staggering, irritabil-

ity, systems depression to the point of coma, and cardiac arrest
can occur.

Barbiturates can cause physical dependence and with it increased tolerance and withdrawal symptoms. Long term users
will often increase their dosage and thus risk the possibility of fatal
reactions.

Cocaine (Coke): Another stimulant derived from the leaves
of the cocoa plant. Cocaine has received renewed attention and
interest among users in the last decade. Cocaine, as a crystalline
powder, is most typically inhaled or snorted, although some
users will inject the chemical. Feelings of pleasure, of adequacy
and of euphoria are reported by users. The euphoria which occurs within a few minutes after inhalation fades quickly and may
be followed by a depression. Continuous sniffing of cocaine may
cause damage to the nostrils and destruction of the nasal mem-
brane. While evidence of respiratory arrest, coma and death has
been reported, this is rarely the case of users who snort. It is
more frequently the result of injection. To date cocaine appears
not to cause physical addiction; however, the powerful compul-
sion to reuse it often results in extreme, and destructive psychological dependency.

Discerning the Why

Perhaps even more essential than knowing the *what* of drug use
is knowing the *why*. Understanding the reason for drug use is essential for appropriate and effective intervention and prevention. Without understanding the need satisfied by the drug, it will be almost
impossible to find more acceptable alternatives.

While there are perhaps as many reasons for drug use as there
are people using such drugs or as there are different effects of the
drugs, the "why" of adolescent drug use can generally be identified
as either *normative use, use as dysfunctional coping,* or *characterological use.* Each type of use, each category of motivation brings
with it unique problems to be faced by youths and their parents and
requires different responses from youth ministers.

Drug Use as Normative. As previously noted, ours is a drug culture. A subtle yet quite pervasive norm within our society is that drug use in a variety of forms (nicotine, alcohol, marijuana, cocaine, prescription tranquilizers, etc.) is acceptable. Whether the message says "Lite tastes great" or "Come up to Salem country," we are surrounded by our heroes and heroines telling us that the way to happiness, success and most definitely acceptance is through the selection of the appropriate brand of alcohol or cigarettes.

The same cultural message pervades the culture of our youth. Added to these more widespread influences are those found in the various video, movie, or rock music offerings which glorify the use of "uppers," "downers" and "in-betweeners." For many if not most adolescents, their initial encounters with drugs came as a result of these various "normative" influences. Peer pressure, fear of exclusion or the excitement of doing what "grown-ups do" provides the basis for initial adolescent experimentation. Adolescent usage of alcohol and tobacco, for example, has been found to be greater among those adolescents whose parents make regular use of these substances.

This is an important point to remember, since many parents are unaware of the "modeling" influence of their own behaviors. Further, these same parents, if they do perceive the "double message" of "Do what I say, not as I do," may often translate their uneasiness into disciplinary responses to their children's abuse. Just as parents need to understand that youths who are experimenting with a soft drug because of the desire to be accepted need not be rushed off to a drug rehabilitation center, parents must also come to grips with the mixed messages they are sending their children regarding drug use.

Youths who have used or experimented with drugs as part of their developmental curiosity and their desire for social acceptance need to be viewed in light of their generally healthy developmental pattern. Youths engaged in drug use because of peer pressure or the desire to be accepted need a trusted advisor who can help them clarify their own insecurities and need for acceptance and to begin to develop alternative ways to gain such acceptance.

One of the first steps in this process is to raise adolescents' awareness of the need being expressed and to highlight for them the subtle pressures and subliminal messages which often impact their "desire" to drink, smoke, etc. From experience, it would seem that these youths who are motivated to demonstrate their independence and their "self-direction" are often moved to resist these subtle pressures once they become aware of them. As such it might be a good idea as a part of ministry/counseling to have adolescents review TV commercials, rock videos, magazine ads, and song lyrics in order to extract the subtle connections being made between drug use (be it nicotine, alcohol, caffeine and the various street drugs) and other, desirable states, such as high esteem, acceptance, athletic/social/sexual prowess, money and a variety of forms of power, etc. Seeing themselves as potentially controlled by these subtle suggestions often acts as a motive from which youths resist the employment of such drugs.

Many youths, however, "buy" the messages conveyed and firmly believe that drug use is the key to acceptance and success. In working with these youths one must completely understand the strength of the need for acceptance to effectively intervene with them. It might be tempting to say to a youth: "Look, you know better. Just say to those offering you drugs, "I am me and I respect my body too much to take these drugs—so if you want me to be a friend, O.K., but not drugs." However, to do so would be quite naive, and perhaps completely ignorant and insensitive to the real social pressure experienced by the youth. To take such a stance against their peers requires them to be willing to stand up and go it alone. Rejection is a painful, often paralyzing experience. The adolescent facing rejection as the alternative to drug use will require more than just a pat phrase or "knowing what is right." He or she will need support and guidance in order to be able to resist the invitation to drugs. He or she will need to be helped to say "no" to the drug, while still saying "yes" to group membership.

In attempting to help youths resist the social pressures, one can be of assistance to by helping them to identify "face-saving" techniques, which will allow them to remain "in" while disengaging themselves from drug use. For example, in working with Charlie, a sixteen year old who neither liked to drink nor wanted to, but was faced by the pressure from his friends who often wanted to buy "quarts of beer" and cruise around in Charlie's car, an attempt was made to have Charlie assert himself. However, it failed because of Charlie's own personal insecurities which supported his fear of losing his friends should he express his anti-drinking feelings. Another approach was possible, though. Through a discussion with Charlie it was discovered that his father had the same aversion to alcohol that Charlie did. In fact, his dad was so sensitive to beer that just the smell of it made him ill. From this discussion Charlie realized that he could tell his friends that drinking in the car was out since "the old man has a nose like a bloodhound." While most of his friends grumbled about Charlie's restrictions, they could identify and could accept the pressure he was under from his "supersnoop" parent.

While it would have been much more mature, and much more desirable, to have Charlie simply assert his own values and stand up against his peers for what he felt was right, the reality was that Charlie was not ready nor able to do this. The possibility of his father's discovery gave Charlie the initial basis from which to say "no" to drinking without risking the loss of his friends. From this "safe" position, Charlie and his counselor continued to work on his self-esteem and assertive rights in order to eventually arrive at a position from which Charlie could say to his friends: "No thanks, I don't like drinking!"

Saying "no" to drug use and even "no" to those advocating drug use will be much easier if the adolescent feels supported and accepted by a group of peers who similarly hold to a non-drug use "norm." The youth minister may be able to play an effective role in the development and coordination of such youth groups by organizing social events (dances, ski trips, athletic competitions, etc.) and encouraging church and civic groups to provide resources for the meetings and activities of groups such as the CYO, or Young Christians, or Teens Opposed to Drugs, etc. These groups have abstinence as their standard or norm. Adolescents who know they can be accepted in another peer group will be less fearful of standing up and expressing their own values, even when such values run contrary to the group with whom they are involved. Further, when such self-expression is done assertively, rather than apologetically (implying guilt or low self-esteem) or demandingly (requiring all the others to follow), then the youths may realize that their abstinence will be accepted even among their original group of friends, and that such personal strength may even be modeled by others in that group.

Being the trusted advisor is a role which needs to be developed and nurtured by the youth minister, for youths involved with drug use and decisions regarding drug use need to have a sounding board which will help them clarify personal needs and concerns and find alternative means for satisfying these needs and addressing their concerns.

Drugs as a Form of Dysfunctional Coping. While initial curiosity, experimentation or peer pressure may lay the foundation for drug use, often other motives support the continued use of drugs. For some adolescents, drugs represent a boost or buffer for their own weak ego and negative self-concepts. Such individuals often find the drug providing the boost or support they need to function socially, or the relief they need from the ongoing pain which accompanies such a poor self-concept.

Youths, for example, who feel sexually inadequate and are paralyzed by fear of rejection may find that a "few belts of booze" or "a couple of hits on a joint" reduces anxiety to a point wherein they feel confident enough to approach their "dream date" at the dance. Having enjoyed the escape from their debilitating anxiety and with the increased confidence chemically supplied, youths may experience success with the person at the dance and mistakenly attribute it to the use of the drug. Thus repetition becomes easier.

Drug use may also reflect inadequate or dysfunctional attempts to cope with other uncomfortable situations or life experiences. Often drug use is viewed as providing a short-lived escape from depression. Adolescents who feel that their lives are meaningless or hopeless, or those faced with an abusive family situation, may attempt to find escape and temporary relief by "tripping with LSD" or getting "mellow" on barbiturates and alcohol.

For others, use of drugs is often an attempt to express their anger and defiance of family or social pressures. Clearly the children who use drugs to express anger toward their parents' disciplinary actions or as a way of dealing with the feelings they have that resulted from their perception of their receiving unjust treatment need to be helped in a way that differs from those approaches found useful for "experimenters."

Children who find drug use to be a short-cut to anxiety reduction, depression relief, or expression of anger need to be assisted in recognizing that drug use is not a short-cut to relief, but a longer, more ineffective, inefficient mode of dealing with these concerns.

Escape and avoidance through drug use is dysfunctional in that it not only fails to address the problems in order to more permanently remove their ill effects, but quite often leads to an increase in the problem from which we originally wanted to escape.

Youths escaping their own anxieties about the future will find that drug use, while providing temporary relief, interferes with rational decision making and thus not only fails to provide them with the direction they desire but most often debilitates their functioning to the point that more problems and difficulties arise. Adolescents, for example, who find that taking pills is the "only" way to face the boredom of school will, in their drug state, be more inattentive, less involved, and thus less successful in school. The results are that youths are often unclear about what is going on within the class. The increased failure and real lack of understanding only increases the negativity of their school experience, and the cycle continues to expand.

Similarly, when youths feel worthless they will not be able to find comfort or increased self-worth through drug dependence. Instead, ongoing drug reliance will only feed back into the negative self-image which lays the foundation for such depression. It is imperative that the youth counselor confronted by this type of user help such users gain the therapeutic insight which will enable them to recognize the self-defeating nature of drug use as a means of adjustment to their real life problems. Quite often simply being a trusted, caring listener will prove sufficient in assisting youths to come to this awareness. At other times, however, the nature and extent of the underlying problem (i.e., anxiety, depression, anger) is such that professional intervention is required. Under these conditions it is important for the youth minister to be able to help youths and their parents to look beyond the drug use in order to see the underlying "pain" and to encourage them to seek out the needed professional treatment. In such an instance, the youth minister may be called upon to provide the family with recommendations and referral and will most certainly be asked to provide the support they need during the early stages of seeking and getting the needed help.

Drugs as Symptomatic of Characterological Problems. A small yet quite significant group of drug users manifest a long-standing, problematic history in which drug use is only one example of a major personality difficulty. Such youths often present themselves as being impulsive, pleasure-seeking, self-centered youths who have demonstrated repetitive and persistent patterns of non-aggressive conduct in which the basic rights of others are violated. Often these youths have histories of truancy, running away, lying and stealing. They tend to have difficulty establishing a normal degree of affection or empathy for others as evidenced by their failure to extend themselves to others, or their inability to have and maintain good friends.

For youths in this category, drug use is not merely a means of release or a ticket to acceptance; it is a way of filling in for their own personality deficits. Such serious drug abusers are not easily motivated to change and are in need of intensive assistance. The role of the youth minister may be to help identify such users and assist their parents in seeking more intensive treatment alternatives, such as hospitalization or confrontative treatment communities.

Prevention—The Special Role of Youth Minister

Hopefully, it is clear from the preceding discussion that the first step in any treatment or intervention is one of discernment. Persons in youth ministry, acting as the first line of such discernment, need to assess both the type and the extent of drug use along with the possible underlying motives for drug use.

The extent of drug use and abuse in our culture highlights the fact that case by case intervention will simply not work and that what is needed is that the underlying causes be identified and preventive measures taken to remove these "causes" wherever possible and to provide alternative "solutions" where needed. The role of youth minister as a preventive agent has yet to be completely developed but is one which, in my estimation, provides the most hope.

Facilitating Parenting

Assisting parents to develop the knowledge and skills required of Christian parents may prove to be the starting point for a preventive approach to drug abuse. As a first step in this process it is essential to begin to develop parent-child relationships and family atmospheres which are conducive for open, honest communication, education, and informational exchange. Further, parents need to begin to demonstrate rational value-based decision making. The modeling of such value-based decision making will provide the basis for their youths becoming thinking, caring adults who will be able to weigh the consequences of their actions and make sound decisions regarding drug use.

Parents seeking to develop the needed skills may rely on the persons in youth ministry as agents of support. For these parents, the youth minister can serve as a valuable resource in communication training (they may really need to learn to listen), value clarification (i.e., unconditional love), and information acquisition (they will need facts about the drugs and drug utilization; information can be found by contacting their childrens' schools, local mental health and mental retardation agencies, and by simply looking in the yellow pages under "Addiction," "Drug Abuse," "Alcoholism," and "Drug and Alcohol Centers" or by contacting the local Public Health Office).

In addition to such training and information gathering, parents concerned about the *possibility* that their child may become involved with drugs need to be encouraged to:

- assess their own double standards regarding drug/alcohol use and begin to model responsible behavior;
- begin to understand the needs of their children and the value often served by drug use (e.g., curiosity, acceptance, getting "in," escape from low self-esteem, etc.);
- learn not to over-react, panic or blame themselves but begin to identify the actual nature, extent and type of problem they may be confronting;
- identify the community resources available to them and their children for drug education, drug treatment and alternatives to drug utilization.

The youth minister's "preventive potential" does not stop with his or her support of the parents' desire to learn more about drugs. There is also a need to take action to encourage parents to become more "responsible hosts." All too often parents fail to provide the needed supervision at youth gatherings. There is a need to establish a social environment in which parents agree not to serve or allow alcohol or other drugs to be used at their houses. Similarly, the youth minister can use information nights, support groups, workshops, etc., to encourage parents to minimize the chances of abuse, even in those situations where alcohol consumption is legal, by providing food and a limited amount of activities such as dancing, gaming, etc.

For those parents who find themselves already in the grip of a crisis in which a youth is experimenting or using drugs, there is a need to help them to relax and not panic. If it is a problem to be dealt with, ignoring it or becoming hysterical will obviously not provide the solutions we seek. Helping the parent to identify the nature of the involvement and the extent of its severity will not only provide us with a direction of intervention but will *prevent* the parent and child from entering into a destructive interaction which may foster the development of drug utilization.

Perceiving youths as an "addicts" because they smoked a "little grass" may create a condition of stress, distrust, and oppression which encourages them to seek further involvement with drugs as a means of escape or a means of expressing their resentment. Parents found in the grips of such a drug crisis need to be encouraged to provide strong yet loving parental authority. They should be assisted in setting reasonable, firm limits for their children while at the same time providing them with unconditional love and ample opportunity for self-expression and decision making. Being able to calmly accept the information their children share, while discussing realistically the possible results and consequences of pro-drug decisions, is again not only an important intervention but a means of prevention.

Preventive Education

In addition to providing youth with drug-free social interaction, youth ministers can help adolescents to become knowledgeable about drug use, its short and long term effects and the special mixing of the adolescent psyche with the effects (both "good" and bad) of particular drugs. Such information will provide them with a basis for understanding the decisions they can make and the consequences of these decisions. Youth ministers may find that such information can be provided within the context of "discussion groups," "rap sessions" and "adolescent information nights" in which youths dialogue with each other in the presence of "an expert" in an atmosphere of trust and loving concern.

Facilitating Healthy Functioning

The youth minister needs to consider ways and means of fostering a youth's development toward self-acceptance and self-esteem. The youth who has developed a healthy sense of self, and who perceives his or her body as valuable and sacred, will view drug inclusion as undesirable if not outright aversive.

Further, adolescents need to recognize the "needs" being satisfied by drug use so that, with the help of a youth minister, alternative, healthier strategies for satisfying these needs can be found. This can be accomplished by organizing teen groups and activities or by providing programs which will help adolescents develop those behaviors which will reduce the need for and likelihood of their ongoing drug involvement. The creation of social groups which provide drug free recreation such as dances, skate parties, ski trips, nights at the movies, etc., and which publicly espouse a norm of drug freeness, will not only provide youths with an alternative social group in which to find acceptance, but will provide the social pressure to reinforce a drug-free value system. The adolescent finding acceptance within such social groups will be less likely to feel unacceptable and thus less likely to seek support or escape through drug use.

Concluding Thoughts

Perhaps we are, as many believe, in the grips of a modern epidemic. The epidemic, however, is not simply one of drug use. It is an epidemic of much deeper and broader consequence.

Our culture has become the culture of ready and instant solutions. It is a culture of immediate gratification and a "live for the moment" attitude. Within this milieu, adolescents are introduced to the magic of chemical solutions.

Whether it be seeking self-stimulation or escape from one's own life problems, the culture appears to call us all to "drink" this, "smoke" that or "pop" this.

Drugs, like all things created, can serve a useful purpose. Their use, and consequently their abuse, needs to be guided by responsible decision making. Everyone in youth ministry needs to respond to this "call for help" by assisting both adolescents and their parents to learn to discern useful from harmful drugs, use from abuse, and effective from ineffective strategies for need satisfaction.

Sources for Further Information

In addition to city, state and federal Mental Health and Mental Retardation Centers, Drug, Alcohol, and Public Health Agencies, and Departments of Health and Education, the following private agencies provide a variety of educational materials.

Hazeldon Educational Materials
Box 176, Center City, Minn. 55012

Public Affairs Committee
381 Park Ave. South
New York, N.Y. 10016

Sunburst Communication
Dept. AW, 39 Washington Ave.
Pleasantville, N.Y. 10570

Chapter 7

Nurturing the Adolescent Through School and Other "Inconveniences"

"Once upon a time, there was a family called 'Nofault.' The Nofaults had three children: Tommy 15, Kathy 10, and Mark 3. Mr. and Mrs. Nofault were happy and quite proud of their family. Tommy was an honor student, who willingly did his homework, cleaned his room and volunteered to do housework on the weekends. Kathy was a child who always cooperated with her mother and father, enjoyed helping with Mark, and never complained when her parents would have to say 'No' to one of her requests. Mark, while only 3, had already exhibited the wonderful traits of his two older siblings. Mark would pick up the toys from his bedroom each evening prior to going to sleep, gleefully took his evening bath, and was always ready and willing to help mom and dad should they ask him for a 'favor.' The family truly enjoyed one another, never argued or fought, and never had a cross word with one another."

Perhaps the only thing missing from the above "fairy tale" is "And they lived happily ever after." Most certainly the aforementioned was a "fairy tale." Families without conflict are non-existent. I am sure that even the Holy Family had its share of conflicts and child crises.

While it is most likely obvious that tales of families without conflict are fantasy, what may not be so obvious is that families who experience conflict can still "live happily ever after." Conflict need not be destructive. Families and individuals can use conflict as a point for growth and increased intimacy. The negativity and destruction which often result from family conflict appears to be less a result of the conflict itself and more a result of the "poor," improper, non-facilitative handling of the conflict.

The current chapter focuses upon a number of the more common areas of conflict and suggests that as youth ministers your role

97

may be to assist families in the use of Christian discipline and appropriate conflict resolution.

"What Happened?"

My years as a parent and a clinician counseling parents and their children have helped me to appreciate that the role of parents is one in which parent priorities and values are often easily subverted and confused. While working with families in crisis, in which there are intense negative feelings and often overt aggression between parents and adolescents, I often find myself asking: "Where has the initial excitement, joy and wonderment, which these parents surely felt upon the birth of this child, gone?" "How does the joy, the love, the bond, get buried over the years, to the point where often hostility and conflict appear in its place?"

It appears that all too often the daily "tasks" of parenting, such as teaching children proper table manners, reviewing the "ABCs" or geometry homework, supervising room clean up, or monitoring a youth's curfew, take center stage. As such, "parenting" often results in pushing to have the task completed at the expense of the love and joy originally felt when introduced to the miracle of life. I can remember my own situation in which one evening, as I was reading the paper, Drew, my middle son, interrupted me asking if I would like to see his homework. Drew's expression told me that he was quite proud of his homework and that he wanted to share his own pleasure with me. In the process of checking the homework I noted that the original question asked for multiple responses and that Drew, while giving an excellent response, offered only a single answer. Forgetting the real task at hand, which was to affirm my son and share in his sense of satisfaction, I became sidetracked by the "task" of getting the "correct answer." Soon my distraction and concern became suggesting, and suggesting became insisting, and my insisting was about to be elevated to threats of reprisal. Luckily I was able to hear myself becoming engaged, quite negatively, in a struggle, that really was not needed, nor desired. I stopped in mid-yell and apologized to Drew for getting so annoyed. I told him that I was not only pleased with his excellent answer but quite proud of his self-direction in doing the homework. While being affirming, I also noted my concern that the teacher may be looking for more than one excellent response, but we would have to wait to see if that were so, since it was clear that he felt as strong about his position as I felt about my own.

What almost became a major conflict and clash of wills ended in an enjoyable, renewing exchange between father and son. While I would like to pretend that such is always the case, the truth is that it is not. And I, like many if not most parents, allow the tasks of my parenting to often distract me from the real responsibility of parenting—to love and to teach the love of God to my children.

As stewards over children's early experiences, parents are responsible to set goals and standards for them. Such goals are often in contrast to those established by the youths themselves. It is the push-pull of these diverse goals, needs and interests and/or diverse means to goal satisfaction which often provides the basis for the destructive conflict exhibited between parent and adolescent. In light of this, parents need to often be assisted to (1) identify their needs/ goals, (2) reassess the importance and value of these goals vis-à-vis the overall impact and consequence of this conflict, and (3) develop strategies for conflict resolution which encourage a no-lose outcome.

The Changing Need for Rules

Understanding the adolescent and his or her changing need for rules, as well as the parents' need for setting guidelines, is often the first step in conflict resolution. The early years of life require that parents exert increased control and set secure, clear limits for the safety of the child. With maturity, the child's own striving for self-direction may begin to conflict with the parents' own "habit" of imposing limits and control. From birth, children have been "dependent" upon parents for direction, control, support and sanction for their action. Increasingly, however, these same children have been attempting to resist parental control and to apply self-direction. Such self-direction may exhibit itself in any number of ways such as children's refusal to eat their peas or the desire to select the clothes to be worn on the first day of school.

The first time a child "challenges" the parents' dictates often comes as a shock (i.e., when a pre-schooler, upon being told to pick up his toys, responds with a "no" or a "not now"). Quite often the clash of needs (for the parent, to clean the room, and for the child, to continue watching his favorite TV show) results in the increase of force from the parents' side—"Do it or else" as the response, or "Because I said so" as the justification.

The "I said so," combined with an increase in the tone of voice or the exhibition of some physical sign of power, may serve well to motivate the child. However, such an approach seems less efficient and effective, and clearly more detrimental, when it is applied to an adolescent. To simply lay down the law or rule with an "iron hand" and assume that it will be effective is to ask for some sort of rebellion, or, maybe even worse, an unhealthy form of acquiescence which stunts the needed natural movement toward autonomy and independence.

On the other hand, when parents reconsider the "issues" and "tasks" over which they are about to battle they may discover that a task ("cleaning the room") is much less important than demonstrating and thus teaching the value of "respect" and "consideration for others." Also, upon closer inspection it may be possible to note that having the task accomplished is not as important as demonstrating a desire to establish a warm, loving relationship and the development of a working, problem solving bond between themselves and their child or adolescent. The point being made here then is that although the raised voice, shaken fist, and threat of punishment may move the child toward the goal of cleaning the room, it may simultaneously move him or her even further away from the more desirable goals of individual, responsible behavior and the maintenance of close, loving relationship.

This is not to imply that extreme permissiveness or lack of limit setting is desirable. Rules need to exist. Knowing the real limits to acceptable behavior and understanding the consequences of violation of these limits is essential to the social and moral development of our youth. Teaching these consequences becomes an important part of the role to be enacted by parents. Yet, what is being emphasized is the parents' need to recognize the importance of self-direction. Adolescents need to sense that while their parents remain responsible for them, and as such need to be involved in setting limits, they are being given opportunities to gain in their own self-control and as such are encouraged and expected to contribute maturely to the development of several limits.

Quite often parents and youth need assistance in developing clarity about their needs and assistance in establishing loving, workable, problem solving bonds. This is not to suggest that youth ministers have to set the correct rules (time the child should come in, length of study time, amount of allowance, etc.) for any specific parent or youth. The specifics regarding the "do's" and the "don'ts" of each rule and regulation need to be left to the individual family with their own unique needs and values. However, the *process* by which rules are developed and implemented are of interest to persons working with youths and their families since the approach taken in understanding and resolving the problem can be more or less facilitative or destructive to the individual's growth and development and the maintenance of a healthy, loving family environment. It is in helping the parents and youths develop facilitative "processes" that those in formal/informal youth ministry may serve an essential role.

The Place of Discipline

Recently at one of the workshops I was giving, a parent raised his hand and asked: "Is discipline in or out this year?" I think I know how he felt and what he meant by his question.

We read so many conflicting reports and we see so many psychologists, social workers, psychiatrists, etc., on TV giving contradictory recommendations on doing this and not doing that. It can be very confusing.

Is discipline in? My response to that parent was: "Discipline has never been out!" His retort, however, cautioned me that much more needed to be said: "Oh great! You mean that now I can go home and beat up my kid for frustrating me?" All too often discipline and punishment are equated. Even though punishment might be considered a disciplining act, it is not a complete definition of discipline and may not even be the most effective tool for discipline. Discipline is *any* kind of experience or training that leads to a correction, modification, molding, or strengthening of a behavior.

Even a cursory consideration of the definition will reveal that discipline is "in" now and has never been out. A boy who modifies his "balance" as a result of falling off his two wheeler has been disciplined by the experience of falling off. Similarly, a woman who adjusts her golf swing because of having sliced the ball on the previous shot has in fact been disciplined by the previous experience. And the young man who begins to change his eating habits, study habits, or room-cleaning behaviors, as a result of some experience—regardless if it is the internal sense of pleasure that comes with better grades, losing weight or having a clean room, or the praise from his parents, teachers or peers—has been disciplined.

Therefore the question that parents need to have answered is *not* whether it is "O.K." or "not O.K." to discipline, but rather how they should, as Christian parents, effectively discipline their children so that what is corrected, modified, strengthened or trained is aligned with their own Christian values and their desired goals for parenting.

Importance of Attitude

As a tool of training or teaching, the discipline process requires that the disciplinarian possess a facilitative attitude and style and effective, appropriate skills. There are a number of excellent parent training, skill development texts written on the topic of behavior modification and discipline. Persons in youth ministry naturally should acquaint themselves with this material. (To assist in this matter a list of recommended sources has been included at the end of this chapter.)

This literature, however, often fails to discuss the important role which parental attitudes and style play in effective, Christian parenting. Parents, while often understanding the concept of effective discipline, fail in their attempts at implementation because of their own ineffective parenting style or the dysfunctional and debilitating attitudes they have about children and the child rearing process.

By accident or design parents have come to hold or share a number of attitudes and beliefs which, when used to guide their behavior, most often prove counterproductive, or dysfunctional. For example, many parents *firmly* believe that children *must* respect them, *must* tell the truth, *must* do homework, *must* . . . *ad infinitum.* And so many parents, myself included, impose a lot of "musts" and "shoulds" on their children. Our children's failure to comply with these "shoulds," "oughts" and "musts" is often the basis for destructive parent-child conflict. Parents, for example, who truly and somewhat rigidly believe that children *must not* question their parents, may find that they are infuriated by their adolescent's "challenge" or "questioning" of a parental rule or dictate. Perceiving children as bold and arrogant for "violating" this "essential" human rule provokes the parent to a state of increased anger and with it an escalation of the conflict.

In such instances, parents finding themselves confronted with situations need help in recognizing that adolescent questioning is not a refusal to adhere to the 11th commandment, "Thou shalt not question." To accomplish this, parents need to reinterpret their youth's actions as a sign of their growth and development of independence and self-direction. Such reinterpretation may be the essential first step in resolving this specific conflict as well as laying a foundation for prevention of future problems.

In actuality, parents in strife often need to be challenged about their attitudes regarding their adolescent and the way *they must act.* The youth minister as a supportive, non-threatening agent can play a key role in helping parents take this first step of attitudinal evaluation and adjustment by providing them with accurate information regarding adolescent development, and by gently confronting their ineffectual attitudes.

One somewhat shocking technique which I have found effective for both parent and adolescent is to announce to them (often in the heat of their own argument about what the child should do, or what dad is being asked to allow) that *there is absolutely nothing that a child or, for that matter, a parent must do!*

To say that such a comment is met with somewhat of a stir of disbelief is putting it mildly. After the initial shock and murmuring die down, the parents will often challenge my statement by pointing out that all children *must:*

   . . . love their parents;
   . . . respect their parents;
   . . . pay taxes;
   . . . die!

Allowing for the fact that many people certainly do believe that these things are absolute necessities, or obligations, I then will encourage the adolescent and his or her parents to reconsider, along with me, these and other such *musts*. On closer inspection we soon begin to understand that each of the above represents a *desirable* action, but that none of the above are absolute, life-determining "musts." If people are willing to take the consequences they can, for example, choose not to pay taxes. People do not cease to exist if they refuse to pay taxes, and in some cases they may even find a way to survive quite comfortably, out of jail, if their morals and their actions allow, or in jail, should their values "justify" the refusal to pay taxes. Similarly, while it is desirable to love one's parents, the reality is that many do not, with the only real consequence being the loss of contact with one or two individuals with whom they could have had shared affection.

The point of this discussion with parents and adolescents is to help them recognize that what is desirable is really a function of what the individual sees as desirable, approachable and motivational. Thus, for those who ascribe to the value of Christian living, following the ten commandments is a "must," in that it is the prescription for achieving our self-ascribed goal of Christian life. And so, in attempting to teach an adolescent to follow these same ten commandments, it might be more helpful to highlight or in some way provide our "student" with insight into the value and role to be played by following such dictates than by simply demanding that he or she *must* follow a certain set of rules.

Again the point of the discussion is not so much to cause a stir, but to have parents, as well as their children, begin to appreciate that everyone does things because of personal needs and the desire to satisfy these needs. If parents, teachers or youth ministers are to be effective in motivating youths to seek the same goals which they feel to be so desirable, then they need to truly understand and appreciate that adolescents do *not* have to take out the trash, do homework, go to school, respect parents, or go to church, even though they will most certainly experience some potentially negative consequences if they don't. Consequently, demanding then will probably not affect our adolescents' motivations or adherence to our preferred ways of acting, but effective teaching and disciplining might. To fully appreciate this, one must still recognize that the parents' realities may be different from the adolescents'. For instance, the trash in the kitchen may be an irritation to the parents and thus they may want it removed. However, their children may be unaffected by its presence (that is, the trash is not piled to the level where it bothers them); as a result, they won't be motivated to remove it. To prevent unnecessary friction there should be an awareness of this rather than the parents holding onto the erroneous belief that once the garbage reaches a certain level everyone—especially their adolescent—should be motivated to remove it.

While at first glance the discussion up to this point may appear to be a simple semantic manipulation, the reality is that language reveals beliefs, and it is our beliefs which affect our emotions and behaviors. Thus believing that "my son *must* take out the trash or clean his room" creates a condition in which I place the entire responsibility of room cleaning, etc., upon my son and I elevate the importance of room cleaning to a level of *essential* rather than simply *desirable*. With this belief, I find myself sitting back waiting for my son to perform his "natural obligation" while I become outraged when he refuses.

If, however, I can alter my belief to reflect a shift from "he has to" to "I would like him to," then I find that I take more responsibility for motivating my son to do what *I* want, rather than what *he* should, and I take less offense at his resistance, remembering that it is I who want, not he; and, like me, he will resist doing anything which he does not want to do.

Once I can effectively switch my attitude regarding such motives, then I come face to face with the problem of how I learn to motivate my children to do things I feel are valuable for them but for which they do not share the same need. Quite often parents wanting to answer these questions will need assistance in developing effective *skills* of discipline.

Skills and Guidelines

Once parents exhibit a functional attitude about motivation and discipline, the youth minister can assist them in employing the skills for effective disciplining. These skills can be conceptualized as the "five C's". To be effective in their disciplining parents need to be *Clear*, use *Cues* and *Consequences*, be *Consistent*, and remain *Calm*. Each of these "guidelines" is important and needs to be discussed and "taught" to the parent.

The first rule or guide in setting limits for a child is for disciplinarians, be they a teacher or a parent, to be *clear* and concise in identifying the specific behavior or rule being addressed. All too often rules are established which are vague and open to much misunderstanding. Telling an adolescent to be home at a reasonable hour, and then getting furious because the youth's definition of reasonableness is different than one's own, makes no sense whatsoever. On the other hand, being overly legalistic can be a trap as well. Instead it is important that parents attempt to be clear in their communication so that both they and their youth know exactly what has been decided.

The second C suggests that parents provide *cues* as to what they are asking for and what will result. If the goal is to teach self-discipline, then children will need to know how to anticipate consequences of their actions and how to internalize these consequences as a source of internal control and direction. For example in teaching a ten month old not to touch the wall outlet, a parent may approach the child, shaking a finger back and forth and saying "No! No!" This visual and verbal cue might then be followed by a tap on the child's hand (i.e., the consequence). The "No! No!" and the shaking finger will act as cues to allow the child to anticipate that should he or she continue touching the socket, then a smack on the hand might result. If one continued to watch this child after he or she received a couple of warning "cues" and smacks, one may begin to notice that as he or she approaches the socket he or she might shake his or her head in a no, no fashion and withdraw the hand. As such the verbal cue has taken on a new meaning and provides the child with internal control. Likewise the parent who fails to "warn" a child prior to that youth's decision is not helping him or her to make responsible, consequential decisions.

Adolescents who are crossing the boundary from being assertive to being disrespectful need to be cued that their behavior is becoming unacceptable if they are to learn to modify and correct that behavior. When a conflict is escalating, then a parent can assist the adolescent in learning self-discipline by "warning": "That's enough," or "You are approaching the forbidden zone," or "Let's cool it," or some other phrase that signifies that the adolescent needs to consider his or her action and make an appropriate decision in order to experience the desired outcome.

It is this outcome or *consequence* which is then our third "C." Most of us are familiar with grandmother's principle which is: "Eat your greens and then you can have dessert." Similarly, many of us have learned to make decisions about less than desirable actions (such as eating our greens) because of the consequence that such an action would have (getting dessert).

When children are small, most parents are more than willing to provide their child with hugs, pats, kisses, smiles, treats, etc., as rewards for doing something which the parent values or desires, such as when the child takes the first step or helps with the dishes. By the time the child reaches adolescence, many parents fool themselves by assuming that the youth no longer wants, needs nor deserves such rewards for doing what they, the parents, value or desire. The reality is that behaviors which are followed by pleasing outcomes will tend to be repeated and to be viewed more positively in and of themselves. Therefore to teach (i.e., discipline) the adolescent to perform a certain behavior, such as to come in on time or to cooperate with the trash detail, it behooves parents, as teachers, to follow the performance of these behaviors by some reward—be it increased free time, the use of the car, a night off from doing the dishes, staying out or up later, etc.

In working with these parents there is a need to recognize that quite often it is the parents' *belief* that the child *should* or *must* perform this or that act that prevents them from using such rewards as motivators. As noted in the previous section such an attitude or belief is both ill-founded and dysfunctional and needs to be addressed if parents hope to become more effective disciplinarians.

It is in this area of discussing consequences that parents will often ask about the use of punishment as a means of "teaching the rules." Parents often rely too heavily on punishment as the consequence to be employed. In the spirit of St. Paul, there is a need to warn parents of the negative effects of such heavy reliance on punishment as a method of discipline: "Parents, don't keep on scolding and nagging your children, making them angry and resentful. Rather, bring them up with the loving discipline the Lord himself approves, with suggestions and godly advice" (Eph 6:4).

With adolescents, parents often employ grounding or confining as a tool of control. Research, and most certainly your own personal experiences, demonstrate the limited effectiveness of such a procedure. If for example the offense continues and the grounding becomes inordinate, then the threat of future grounding means nothing. ("I am already grounded all year, so who cares?") Furthermore, the adolescent may soon come to discover that it is easier to escape (run away, sneak out, etc.) than to endure the grounding. Because of the intrinsic difficulties in the use of punishment I suggest that if punishment is to be used, it should be used only rarely and only in a mild form. Since the benefit of punishment is in its temporary suppression of the undesired behavior, any hopes of changing the behavior will necessitate that punishment be accompanied by an opportunity to perform the desired behavior and a reinforcement for such performance. As such I often explain to parents that when they employ punishment, such as grounding, it would prove more effective if they also informed their adolescents that doing this or that (a desired behavior, such as cleaning their room or washing the car) will serve to work off the punishment. Through this coupling the youth will come to value the desired behavior as having led to some desirable outcome (removal of punishment).

Helping parents to recognize the value and power of their word of praise, or their providing of a small privilege or reward, in the process of teaching their youths to perform the desired behavior is a difficult yet essential task for the youth minister.

The fourth and perhaps one of the most important guidelines to communicate to parents is the need to be *consistent*. This does not mean that they have to be rigid, unchanging and 100% consistent, but rather that the rules, the cues, and the consequences they create be consistent and not merely a function of their own mood or whim.

Consistency allows children to make the needed predictions

about their world and its reaction to them. Children who cannot predict their parents' rules or their reaction to rule violations will become anxious with uncertainty and afraid to test any limits in the
process of growing in independence. Or alternatively, parents who
inconsistently react to rule violations may encourage their adolescent to gamble that this or that time he or she will be able to get away
with it. Unfortunately, just as consequences can teach appropriate
behavior, inconsistent parents who encourage their child to gamble
with the rules and who, through their inconsistency, allow the child
to be successful in their violation, will in fact be reinforcing, or teaching the child inappropriate behaviors (e.g., violation rather than adherence to the rules.)

The final C in our guidelines is to help the parent approach the
establishment and enforcement of rules in a *calm* and *caring* fashion.
Of all the lessons parents need to teach children, the most important
is that of love. It is in approaching the adolescent calmly and caringly
that a message of love and concern is conveyed. Children learn love
not by instruction or verbal command but by the modeling they receive at home.

While there is certainly an interest in teaching acceptable, appropriate and desired behavior, one would like to do it in a way that
affirms one's love for the child. Yelling, screaming, attacking and using sarcasm will only teach children that the parent is angry and out
of control and that the parent is rejecting and unaccepting of them.
Quite often the parents' "upset" state distracts the child from the real
lesson to be learned—namely, "I violated a rule, a rule which was
established for my benefit by parents who are attempting to be the
best parents possible because of their love for me!"

The Significance of Style

Parents attempting to integrate the effective skills of the five C's
of discipline, along with a functional, Christian attitude, are often in
need of an appropriate model to emulate. There is no better model
of effective disciplining then Christ. The example provided by Christ
often proves quite helpful in assisting parents to intergrate an effective disciplining attitude and skills with their own parental style. A

primary lesson to be gained from reflecting on Christ as model is that one teaches first, and foremost, by example. Christ set before his disciples not just instruction, but a living example of his instruction.

The importance of style and modeling cannot be overemphasized. Parents need to be helped to consider their own parenting style and the messages such a style may be conveying to their child. For example, parents who employ an *autocratic* style in which obedience and blind acceptance is valued above all employ punitive, coercive, forceful methods for rule implementation and restrict verbal give and take between themselves and their child. They may have their rules followed, but at what cost?

Youths reared in such an environment not only learn the rules but also learn to use force as a method of need satisfaction. These youths learn to treat others as they have been treated and thus approach others with limited sensitivity, concern or respect for their needs. Further, adolescents with such parental models will find that it is through lying, sneaking and avoiding (e.g., running away) that it is possible to get what they want while avoiding negative consequences.

Research supports that such a parenting style of discipline not only encourages similar attitudes and styles in their youths but also results in the creation of a family with reduced closeness, produces children with low self-esteem and feelings of self-condemnation, and encourages increased power struggles between parent and child. Hostility toward parents, age prejudice, antisocial activities, (such as stealing, lying, fighting and vandalism), feelings of social alienation, rejection of traditional moral standards, and the inability to relate well to other people appear to also result from such a parenting style.

Often parents in an attempt to avoid such negative feelings and interaction with their youth, or because they firmly believe that the child should never be frustrated, swing to a *permissive* style of discipline. Such a style can be as negative in its effects as an autocratic approach. Permissive parents often present themselves as a "friend" of their child, a resource to be used as the child wishes. Such parents abdicate their own responsibility for shaping the child's behavior into socially and morally acceptable patterns. The immediate concern appears to be to free the child from constraint, to avoid conflict—and to be liked!

The lack of control and direction given by permissive parents often results in children having trouble believing that their parents really care about them. "If they truly love me, why would they let me do that which could hurt me?" is often an unspoken question for these children. Moreover, permissiveness often encourages self-centeredness, wherein the primary concern for such youths is doing and achieving their own hedonistic goals. Perhaps even more devastating than the possible negative behaviors which may result from such a style of parenting (e.g., youths who are whining, self-indulging) is that positive, prosocial and ethically motivated behaviors such as altruism, empathy and concern for the needs of others most often fail to develop.

The point to be made is that parents employing either autocratic or permissive styles are doing more harm than good and need to be shown a more effective and facilitative style of parenting.

The youth minister needs to assist parents to see that while Christ could be firm, he was also kind. Firmness in rule setting needs to be tempered with a kindness and concern for the legitimate needs of the other. As such, a parent who can exhibit an authoritative, democratic style of parenting, in which the firmness of an authoritative parent is tempered by the freedom found within a mutually respecting, democratic setting, will find not only that are rules set, and most often enacted, but that the rules and rule setting process become part of the youth's internal standards.

Such a firm and kind position values both the independence of the adolescent and the need for conformity and responsibility. This approach affirms the children's right to their needs and their need satisfaction while at the same time setting a standard for socially appropriate, rationally effective, and morally desirable means of needs satisfaction. From this orientation parents encourage their adolescent to participate in the mutual decision making, while knowing that the ultimate responsibility for the decision is that of the parent.

When effectively implemented, such a style results in the adolescent tending to be much more service-oriented, concerned about the rights and needs of others, free from feelings of alienation and committed to higher ethical and religious standards. The family is often characterized as close, loving, and conflict resolving, and the parents viewed as desirable models.

For such a parent style to exist, parents need to firmly believe in the integrity and the legitimacy of the adolescent's needs while at the same time affirming their own responsibility to guide. This style of parenting requires that parents recognize the inevitability of conflict, in which the needs of one party (either parent or youth) will in some way restrict or prohibit the needs satisfaction of another party. Upon accepting this inevitability the firm and kind parent will develop strategies which encourage no-lose or win-win conflict resolution. Again the youth minister can play an invaluable role as an encourager and enabler of this firm and kind model of parenting as well as a facilitator and teacher of this form of conflict resolution.

Resolving Conflict

Conflict will exist between parent and child anytime one or both parties perceive the existence of incompatible goals, scarce rewards and resources or actual interference from the other party in achieving a particular goal. Thus, the perception of the adolescent who wishes to stay out with friends until midnight, and whose parents' desire to have him or her "safe" and in at eleven, is that his or her goal is not only incompatible with that of the parents but that the parents are interfering with his or her goal attainment. Similarly, those same parents may view the youth's request to stay out until midnight as incompatible with their own need for sleep and comfort in knowing that their son or daughter is home safe. With the incompatibility or at least the apparent incompatibility of needs, conflict may result.

Ironically, often what is perceived as incompatible is not. Parents as well as their adolescent oftentime need assistance in identifying and articulating the real need or desired goal. There is a need on the part of persons in youth ministry to facilitate this identification process along with the development of a mutually satisfying solution. For example, consider the above conflict. While arithmetically it may appear that a solution could be to have the youth come in at 11:30, such a resolution will often prove unsatisfactory to both parties. This solution fails to resolve the real problem. The parents in this example will still feel dissatisfied, being more tired than desired, and the youth still frustrated and embarrassed by having to still leave thirty minutes before the others.

To resolve the apparent conflict the youth minister needs to help the parent and youth to discern that the real need is not eleven or twelve, but the need for the child to feel "adult-like," "conform with the expectations of his peers" and "avoid being embarrassed by having to leave early," and for the parents to feel relaxed, knowing their child is safe.

Once the real needs are identified, a mutually satisfying solution may be determined (for example, as in the situation previously cited, to stay until midnight but the parents will pick the youth up, or to come home at eleven and feel free to save face by "complaining" about the parents). Working toward a mutually satisfying solution requires that those involved not only identify the desired goals but recognize and avoid the pitfalls to successful conflict resolution.

Pitfalls to successful conflict resolution are polarization, win-lose orientation, use of coercion, escalation, and "detouring." Again in youth ministry there is a call to help both parents and youths recognize the manifestation of these roadblocks to successful conflict resolution within their own encounter.

Polarization.   Often, when in conflict, individuals begin to polarize themselves, viewing the other individual's needs as illegitimate, stupid, or simply unimportant. The youth may fail to see the "realness" of the parents' need to feel that their child is safe, or, similarly, the parents may fail to appreciate the importance of their youth's need to be like the crowd. Such illegitimizing will lead to the position in which one party (parent or youth) feels *absolutely* right, and justified in their request, and the other clearly wrong, or silly. From such an orientation "compromise" or attempts at mutual satisfaction will not be considered.

Both the youths and their parents in such an instance need help to step into the perspective of their counterparts so that they can appreciate and accept the legitimacy of the other's needs. If a person can appreciate the need and the right to satisfy the need of the other party, he or she will most likely be more willing to cooperate in strategizing about ways which will be mutually satisfying.

Win-Lose Orientation. We are living in a competitive, win-oriented culture, and quite often, when confronted by conflict, it is "natural" to position oneself to win at all costs even when the costs of winning may be more severe then if we had been more flexible and cooperative. Again the youth minister needs to assist adolescents and their parents to consider cooperation as a strategy for resolving conflict, learning to give and take not only as a way of winning the battle and the war but also as a means of preventing future battles and wars.

Coercion. A major temptation of parents confronting conflict is to run to their position of power and attempt to coerce their child to succumb to their position. Relying on threats of reprisal, fear of punishment, physical threat or guilt ("I said so and I'm your parent") may win the battle but, as we have seen under the autocratic style of parenting, may destroy the relationship and the child.

Escalation. Quite often what starts out as a mild dispute ("I want you to be in at eleven" or "I want you to clean your room now") ends in an explosive exchange. When blocked or thwarted in one's attempt at obtaining a goal (to have my child in at a specific time), an individual may experience frustration and an increase in discomfort. As a result of this frustration and discomfort there is a temptation to heighten one's efforts in order to "push" through or in some way remove the blockage (i.e., an adolescent's resistance to coming in at a specific time). Yet, with the increase in force pushing toward the goal comes an increase in the resistance, thus perpetuating the difficulty.

In the process of escalation, not only energies and employed force go beyond the level needed for resolution of the initial concern, but quite often the original issue and concern will get lost in the heat of the exchange. The emotions have peaked to a point where it is not merely a problem with need satisfaction; it is an all-out attack and counterattack between those involved.

Under these conditions, regardless of the outcome of the conflict, both parties will feel dissatisfied, and the impact on the individual (feeling inadequate, foolish, unlovable, unloved, etc.) or the relationship (becomes something to avoid, not develop) may far outweigh the gains accrued by the conflict. The youth minister working with parents and adolescents in conflict need to help both parties stick to the original issue and reduce the emotional intensity (perhaps by taking a time out, or by removing themself momentarily).

No-Lose Strategies

One strategy for avoiding these pitfalls and achieving successful conflict resolution is through a use of a "no-lose" approach to conflict resolution. While a "no-lose" strategy is difficult if not impossible to always achieve, its potential positive effects makes it worth pursuing as the first approach to conflict resolution.

A "win-win" or "no-lose" strategy requires that the parent and child be willing to sit and (1) clarify and identify their specific needs (not strategies), (2) brainstorm together as many possible strategies for mutual need satisfaction, (3) evaluate the cost and payoffs to each possible solution or strategy, (4) select and implement a strategy on a trial basis, and (5) follow up on the strategy and evaluate its effectiveness by sharing how each other felt about the results of that solution. Such a procedure requires a lot of time and energy on the part of the participants and assumes that mutual satisfaction is possible. When such time and energy are not available, or when the nature of the conflicting needs is such that mutual satisfaction is not possible, attempts at a no-lose situation, even in abbreviated form, can still prove effective.

Parents who employ such a style, when confronted with the reality that no mutually satisfying solution can be found, must take the responsibility for selecting that solution which appears the most satisfying to those involved. Under these conditions the adolescent may protest. But parents taking a no-lose position will be able to make it clear to the youth that they can recognize that this is not a totally satisfying solution to either party, and that they are open to considering any other solution which moves them closer to mutual satisfaction, but at the current time this is the best of all the solutions *they* were able to identify. Such a position will most often leave the youth with the feeling: "I may not like the result, but I have no better alternative, My parents tried to work it out and this is the best *we* could come up with." The frustration of not getting exactly what one wants is part of our human condition, and the youth, knowing that all attempts at cooperation were made, will accept the frustration knowing the love and support of his or her parents.

Concluding Thoughts

"Living happy ever after" need not be restricted to fairy tales or families named "Nofault." Parents who are aware of their adolescent's growing need for independence and self-direction and who are skilled at providing him or her the opportunity and discipline to grow will often find happiness ever after for both themselves and their youth.

Conflicts will exist whenever and wherever individuals with divergent and exclusive needs come face to face. When the conflict is between parent and child the results may prove to be growthful or destructive depending on the skills and attitudes of those involved.

The youth minister working with families in crisis needs to bring to them the skills and attitudes of facilitative, "no-lose" problem solving. With the appropriate skills and attitudes, the directive prescribed by Paul to "bring them up with the loving discipline the Lord himself approves, with suggestions and godly advice" (Eph 6:4) can serve as the substance for their story which will end . . . happily ever after.

Recommended Materials

Becker, W. *Parents Are Teachers: A Child Management Program.* Champaign, Ill.: Research Press, 1971.

Ellis, A., Wolfe, J.L. and Moseley, S. *How To Raise an Emotionally Healthy and Happy Child.* New York: Institute for Rational Emotive Therapy, 1980.

Miller, W.H. *Systematic Parent Training.* Champaign, Ill.: Research Press, 1977.

Mount, G.R. and Walder, S. *The Art and Science of Child Management.* Dubuque: Kendall/Hunt Pub., 1982.

Wagemaker, H. *Parents and Discipline.* Philadelphia: Westminster Press, 1980.

Chapter 8

Loneliness and Alienation:
Adolescent Without Connection

> "I sit in my chair, I'm filled with despair . . . with
> gloom everywhere, I sit and I stare . . . I know that I'll soon
> go mad . . . in my solitude."

Such are the words of the lovely melody of Duke Ellington. Most
certainly "solitude" is not only a beautiful melody, but also a poi-
gnant and painful reflection of the experience of every youth who
feels isolated, alone and alienated.

Relationship and the resulting sense of "connectedness" and social bonding have long been considered to be essential elements of
one's psychological well-being. While such is true for all human
beings, the significance of relationships is clearly highlighted during
the period of adolescence. Every important social relationship
undergoes change during adolescence. Changes in the adolescent's
ongoing relationships with family and friends, as well as new relationships with teachers, employers and other members of the community, require a development of new strategies for interpersonal
relating.

The adolescent is in the midst of a redefinition of self: a redefinition which is responsive to the new social realities. The process of
moving away from family ties, toward a sense of independence and
autonomy, often places the youth in a position of "standing alone."
No longer able to enjoy the security of childhood and yet still excluded from a position in the world of the adult, the adolescent may
feel estranged, truly standing on "the outside looking in."

These feelings of estrangement are part of those normal developmental crises to be resolved by all adolescents; however, for some
the resolution is more or less functional. Youths who arrive at this
"crisis" with a stable sense of self are able to develop a feeling of inner

security and thus know that independence need not be a precursor to isolation. For these youths the peer group, while proving important in their lives, is not viewed as *essential* to their happiness. They see the peer group as offering a base of support and a "laboratory" in which they can develop and practice their new roles as future adults. Experimenting with styles and fashion, minor rebellions and group protest are all reflections of the attempt in adolescence to reconnect to society, in a manner befitting an increased need for autonomy and mature independence.

Many youths, however, who find it difficult to establish a stable sense of self, feel that they are completely out of step and unable to fit in anywhere. Such youths feel isolated from themselves (intrapsychic loneliness), cut off from the world, especially peers (social isolation), and quite often abandoned by God (spiritual loneliness). For this group the need for peer reconnection becomes elevated to the point where the possibility of not gaining acceptance within their peer group produces an overwhelming sense of anxiety. Such youths are often driven to "fit in" at any cost. For these youths the need to belong is at a level of intensity wherein it could accurately be termed "popularity neurosis." Worried that they don't have the right clothes or haircut or aren't doing the "in" things, such concerns are all manifestations of the intense drive to "belong" and are often accompanied by an intense anxiety and devastating fear of the possibility of not being "in." Being left out is exceptionally painful. The misery can be intense, and depression, alcohol use, delinquency, physical illness and suicide may even result.

The experience of being alone, disconnected, isolated and alienated may not only threaten the healthy development of young people but also the health and well-being of their parents as well. The parents, aware of the painful experience of their son or daughter who feels isolated and alone, often feel isolated themselves. Their inability to "connect" with their child in a way that will provide the comfort they so desperately wish to impart is both frustrating and painful.

Adolescents and their parents who are faced with this sense of loneliness and alienation need a connection. The youth minister may be that point of connection.

Loneliness

Loneliness is no stranger. Everyone knows it through direct personal experience or through contact with others in one's daily ministries. But the pain called loneliness is not simply a label for those times or experiences in life when one is alone. It is not that simple loneliness and aloneness are not synonymous. An adolescent, in particular, often needs and wants time to be alone, time to be alone with himself or herself.

Loneliness occurs at those times when one has a feeling of desolation, of isolation, of being cut off and estranged. It may be a feeling of loneliness because of losing a first true love and "knowing" that no one could really understand the pain being felt; it may be the more extensive experience of being unable to "relate" or honestly share with parents. Whatever the source though, the adolescent experiencing loneliness is experiencing pain and is often in need of assistance.

The 1978 President Commission on mental health took the position that it is a societal responsibility to provide mechanisms for social integration and stated that a "healthy society provides opportunities for people to connect in (meaningful) ways . . . and provides special help for those unable to avail themselves of such opportunities."

As Christians, "connecting" is more than a good mental health practice; it is a cornerstone of our faith. Relationship and being part of community are not just *desirable* social goals; they are essential to the desire for a personal living out of the imperative of Christian teaching.

The trinitarian doctrine of God emphasizes the value and interest in relationship. As Christian youth ministers, there is a need to address the issue of the isolated and lonely youth, not simply as a concern for their mental health, but as a reflection of one's own ministry and desire to facilitate the youth's response to Christ invitation: "Come, follow me."

There are numerous causes for the experience of loneliness. Albeit each cause requires a specific intervention, the two most common contributors to loneliness for the adolescent are the youth's lack of social skill and limited opportunities for social contact. Given this problem, hopefully, the youth minister may be in a position to facilitate the acquisition of such social skills and restructure church, family and community networks in order to provide youths experiencing difficulties with increased opportunities for social contact.

Skills

Quite often the lonely, isolated youth has failed to develop the necessary prerequisite skills for gaining admission and acceptance into the peer group. While there is no one generally accepted model, theory or program for social skills training, a number of excellent approaches have been developed and should be considered by the youth minister. Workshops, training sessions and specific educational programs designed to teach assertiveness skills, interpersonal problem solving, conflict resolution and other essential social skills have been used clinically for the purpose of assisting adolescents to overcome their deficient social skills. (Such material is beyond the scope of the current work, and the reader who is interested in pursuing this topic is referred to the suggested readings listed at the end of the chapter.)

Even when such sophisticated and elaborate training models are beyond the resources or interest of the youth minister, they may still provide a valuable skills training service by simply teaching the youth the basis for good, active, empathetic listening and simple, descriptive disclosure. A number of the techniques discussed in Chapter 3 would be of value for the adolescent desiring to learn more effective communication.

Opportunity

In addition to assisting in the development of the necessary social skills, the youth minister can assist the isolated and lonely youth to find opportunities for social contact.

As agents of a variety of institutions—churches, schools, hospitals, etc.—youth ministers need to begin to consider questions such as "How do we foster adolescent contact?" and "How might we begin to restructure these social opportunities to facilitate increased inclusion among all members?"

In responding to the above questions or felt deficiency, one should be cautioned in providing for adolescent peer contact by attempting to develop specific "making friends" types of encounters. The research on social inclusion and relationship building has demonstrated that such gatherings often elevate the debilitating anxiety of the adolescent and result in increased social inhibition and withdrawal. This same literature, however, points to the fact that where the primary focus of the gathering is on the completion of a task or a project, then increased belongingness is an "unitentional" yet quite desired side-effect. Projects, tasks or interactions which require those involved to share a common goal and work together for its achievement not only increase the interdependence among members but also result in an increasing approachability and inclusion among members.

As youth ministers there is a need to review the social activities provided in one's churches, schools, and social agencies, and ask:

"Do these activities foster interdependence, or competition?"

"Do they require or encourage social interaction, or isolation and self-centeredness?"

"How can they be modified so as to encourage interaction and interdependence?"

The Role of Family

The family is one social institution which, with some modification, can serve to reduce the negative impact of loneliness. The family can function as (1) a direct source of interpersonal involvement, (2) a context for the acquisition of interpersonal skills and facilitative attitudes, and (3) a secure base from which to establish peer relationships.

In working with parents, one should assist them in making the needed modification in their family structure and schedule in order to provide opportunities for their youth's social interaction while at the same time providing the appropriate modeling of social behavior. This is not to suggest that the parents take up the role of friend, but that they begin to consider ways in which they can facilitate the youth's process of interaction with friends.

Parents may facilitate their youth's social contact by opening their house to their adolescent's peer group and by encouraging such gatherings by providing refreshments and interactive entertainment (ping-pong, cards, trivia contests, dancing, or simply a place to talk). Further, parents can increase their child's opportunities for social contact by helping them obtain the resources which they feel are necessary for making contact with their friends, be it a ride to the dance, money for the movie, or freedom to go to the mall.

In addition to increasing their child's opportunities for social contact, parents need to be taught to serve as models of appropriate interpersonal skills and attitudes. Parents who are critical, rejecting, uncaring and unlistening decrease the self-esteem among their adolescents and increase the incidents of loneliness. Teaching parents to be "active listeners," model's of social disclosure, and in general taking an interest in their youth, may facilitate their process of teaching adolescents the use of these same skills in gaining and maintaining the attention of their peers.

Alienation

Quite often the sense of loneliness extends far beyond the failure to connect with this person or group at this particular place and time. Some adolescents experience a total breakdown of their sense of attachment to, and within, society. Alienated youths experience a state of total estrangement between themselves and the world—an estrangement in which they not only feel alone and cut off but also unwanted, unvalued and unloved by all.

The devastation experienced in alienation is reflected by the psalmist:

> Take pity on me, Yahweh.
>   I am in trouble now.
> Grief wastes away my eye,
>   my throat, my inmost parts.
> For my life is worn out with sorrow,
>   my years with sighs;
> My strength yields under misery,
>   my bones are wasting away.
> To every one of my oppressors I am contemptible,
>   loathsome to my neighbors,
>   to my friends a thing of fear.
> Those who see me in the street
>   hurry past me;
> I am forgotten,
>   as good as dead in their hearts,
>   something discarded (Ps 31:9–12).

With complete disconnection, where is one to turn except to Yahweh? But for many youth, Yahweh appears not to want to respond. Adolescents who are alienated feel they are living in a chronic state of disappointment. Alienated youths feel as if they are consistently letting themselves down, always falling short of their own expectations and disappointing others; they see themselves as being unable to meet their demands and ultimately feeling valueless and unworthy of love—even the love of God!

The sense of hopelessness and helplessness which accompanies this alienation seems unremitting. Clearly for such youths the message found in Deuteronomy has little meaning yet is so needed.

> "Though you may have been driven to the farthest corner of the world, even from there will the Lord, your God, gather you; even from there will he bring you back" (Deut 30:45).

Retreat, Rebel, Run Away

While turning outward to others or to God is the prescribed antidote to alienation, most youths react to a state of estrangement by either withdrawing from self, others, and God, or by striking out against themselves, others, or even God.

Many youths attempt to seek relief from their pain by retreatism, a retreatism which directs them to drugs, alcohol, or even suicide in hopes of finding relief. For others the frustration and sense of impotence results in a rage which manifests itself in a rebellious rejection of the mainstream social values and social rules.

This rebellion most often seeks expression through the formulation and acceptance of a divergent set of values and norms and perhaps in alignment with a cult or group which provides a compensatory sense of belonging and an avenue for expression of the impotent rage the youth feels against the mainstream. One of the most common manifestations of this "rebellion" is running away.

There are many possible reasons for running away. Some leave out of a desire for adventure while others are moved by the need to escape a real or perceived "intolerable" home life. For many youths, however, running away is both a manifestation of and a response to their sense of alienation. These youths feel completely ignored and detached from society. They can't communicate with their parents and they feel an impotent rage over what they perceive to be arbitrary injustices. Alienated youths see running away as the only way of expressing their anger and escaping their pain.

Alienated youths whose sense of detachment and rebellious anger drives them to leave the home present a special concern to the youth minister. Cold, scared, without resources, many alienated youths find themselves at the doorstep of a church, parish hall, rectory or some other potential haven. These youths are in crisis. The youth minister confronted by runaways needs to be prepared to assist them and their parents through the crisis.

The First Step—Space and Time

The runaway is usually in a state of emotional and perhaps physical turmoil. Hungry, cold, exhausted, and perhaps ill, the runaway is in need of comfort, not confrontation. Beset with varying degrees of defiance, anxiety, anger and fear, the runaway needs an empathetic, supportive ear and not, at least initially, a lecturette on the ills of running away.

While the above may appear obvious, all too often in our own state of uncertainty we fail to open our hearts and our homes to those in crisis but retreat to moralizing in hopes of letting youths see the wrong they have done.

The beginning of reconnection starts with a friendly encounter. In addition to "welcoming" runaways into one's "haven" and providing for their physical needs, there is a need to offer youths a "recovery period." This is a time for them to gather their thoughts and their energies and a period in which there is an allowance of space and time to begin to understand what they have done and what they need to consider in beginning to make responsible decisions. During this "recovery period" the youth minister needs to listen, to reflect, and most certainly to demonstrate honest, unconditional care and concern. Runaways are quite often confused and unsure about what is going to happen to them. As such they need time, without questions, without challenge and additional concerns, in order to regroup and recover to face the very important issues of reconnecting with self, friends, family and God.

Reconnecting

Once runaways have relaxed and regained both physical and psychological comfort and strength, the process of identifying the "whys" and "wherefores" for running away needs to begin.

Initially, runaways may feel that all has become fused and confused, and that the incidents of the past are only a blur. They are often overwhelmed with the possibilities of what they have done and are unable to place things in perspective. As such it is helpful for them if they can be provided with a clear outline as to what will happen in the next hour or two. While it is essential to let them know that their parents will be contacted, it is just as important to assure them that there is a willingness to wait and provide them some time and space prior to taking this step.

Perhaps in fear of their parents' reaction, the youths need to believe that persons in youth ministry will not only serve as supporters but also as protectors and advocates for them and their concerns. During these early stages of contact it is important to be honest with them and not try to trick or trap them. These youths need to feel connected, respected and cared for, and one's honesty and concern may be the beginning threads of reconnection.

Most youths who run away do not wander far from their home. Experience shows that these adolescents are often seeking to make a statement and not trying to escape. It is important to encourage them to ventilate about their "problems" at home prior to making contact with the family. During this period of "reconnaissance" (that is, problem identification and resource identification) the youth minister needs to affirm the runaways, be supportive of their struggle, and affirm that his or her goal is to be both advocate for them and emissary for their troubled family.

It is during these early hours that the importance of the "helping relationship" becomes evident. While one may be eager to reunite the youth and family and thus solve the problem of the runaways, the real emphasis needs to be on the development of the caring-sharing relationship. The root of their problem is their own frustration and inability to form and maintain a relationship, a connection, and thus it is with relationship that the "cure" needs to begin. Without this foundation of a helping relationship the youth's problems may be exacerbated rather than alleviated.

During these early hours of counseling the youth minister needs to assist the runaways in identifying the specific problems which led to their departure. Similarly, the youths and the youth minister need to begin to identify possible solutions and re-establish confidence and hopefulness in their ability to make productive decisions. The focus throughout such work with runaways should be to encourage them to make free, responsible, decisions.

The youth minister needs to be cautioned against being judgmental. While avoiding being authoritative and judgmental, those in youth ministry need to be the voice of reality for the runaways, helping them see the real implications and consequences of their actions and assisting them in identifying real alternatives. From this perspective the youth minister may need to know about issues of legal status, custody rules, alternative living environments, educational alternatives, etc., for runaways in their community.

Contact

The youth needs to recognize that just as running away was not a solution, nor is simply coming to someone for bread and board.

While persons who deal with youths cannot resolve the problems of adolescence, they are a port in a storm and a link back into a loving relationship. Once the "problems" have been identified, there is a need to identify those conditions, or safety factors, which runaways feel are needed in order to "comfortably" and "willingly" make contact with their family. Quite often the comfort and sense of security experienced within the counseling relationship up to this point will serve as the only condition needed for the youths to reach out and make contact with their parents. Further, at such a point the youth ministers may find it useful to highlight the fact that they will be present and that this counseling setting can serve as the buffer and even the model for productive interaction and contact with their parents.

It is essential to let the youths know that one will be with them throughout the entire journey and that they will not be abandoned once they make contact with their parents.

Regardless of the length of or degree to which the youth minister is involved, one of the most valuable "interventions" to be provided by them is that of returning the family to a working relationship. Quite often the parents, like their child, are angry, resentful, anxious and most clearly confused and uncertain. Questions such as "What went wrong?" and "What are we to do?" are the focus of their concern. The youth minister needs to help the parents begin to answer these questions in a facilitative rather than self-debasing manner.

The parents of a runaway all too often act like "Monday morning quarterbacks," blaming themselves for doing and saying all the wrong things. These parents need to be helped to understand that what appears so clearly to them now was not so clear at the time of their decision and that their decisions were made from a sense of what was best—and with much love.

Like everyone, parents make mistakes. But parents of a runaway need to know that it was not just their mistakes that led to the current state of detachment. They need to know too that their youth is responding to pressures and pushes originating from within himself or herself and from peer demands and not simply reactive to family pressure.

Further, rather than casting fingers at themselves or others for blame, parents need to come to appreciate that it is *now* that we need to begin to establish the important family ties. Parents need to be encouraged to open their arms in support and love, and to open their minds in a special willingness to work at resolving the conflict between themselves and their child. Helping a parent move from self-accusation ("It's all my fault") or a position of condemnation ("Damm kid . . . after all we did!") to one of joyful hope ("Let us eat and celebrate because this son of mine was dead and has come back to life. He was lost and is found"—(Lk 15:23) is the essential first step in having their child respond: "I will break away and return to my father" (Lk 15:18)

Referral—Ongoing Help

Sometimes the negativity existing between parent and child or the complexity of the problems underlying the reasons for running away are such that the youth minister feels ill-prepared to working with the child or his or her family. Under these conditions it is important for the youth minister to continue to act as an advocate for the child and an emissary for the family by working with them to make contact with professionals trained to work with such families. The youth minister facing such a situation may want to highlight the value of their own "relationship" for bringing the family closer as a model for the value of ongoing family counseling.

Concluding Thoughts

Adolescents are by definition breaking with the old, in hopes of emerging in the new. Pushed and pulled to a new identity, a new sense of self, adolescents may find themselves at odds with the mainstream. Feeling estranged, disconnected from their family, their friends, and perhaps even their God, many youths attempt to run and to escape.

Youth ministers are called by their ministry to reflect the Church's mission of *koinonia* by establishing fellowship and community. Lonely and alienated adolescents need both the skills and the opportunity for connecting. For this group, the youth ministers' efforts to reach out and connect not only are desirable but are actually an essential component of their ministry.

Reference

Rook, K.S. "Promoting Social Bonding." *American Psychologist* 39 (1984) 1389–1407.

Recommended Materials

Adler, R.B., Rosenfeld, L.B. and Towne, N. *Interplay.* New York: Holt, Rinehart and Winston, 1980.

Burns, D.D. *Intimate Connections.* New York: Morrow, 1985.

Egan, G. *Face to Face.* Monterey: Brooks/Cole, 1973.

Gesten, E.L. *et al.* "Promoting Peer Related Social Competence in Schools." In M.W. Kent and J.E. Rolf (eds.), *Primary Prevention of Psychopathology,* Vol. 3: *Social Competence in Children.* Hanover, N.H.: University Press of New England, 1979.

Oden, S. and Asher, S.R. "Coaching Children in Social Skills for Friendship-Making." *Child Development* 48 (1977) 495–506.

Spivack, G., Platt, J.J. and Shure, M.B. *The Problem-Solving Approach to Adjustment: A Guide to Research and Intervention.* San Francisco: Jossey-Bass, 1976.

Chapter 9

Suicide: The Darkest of All Moments

> Pushed to the edge of despair, the young man felt his heart to be nearly broken with sorrow. He asked that his friends stay by his side for just a little while. But they, like many of the others, seemed to abandon him. They could not stay with him even for an hour.

The story line is neither well disguised, nor should it be. Christ, in showing us his humanity, felt the pains, the disappointments, and the frustrations which life often has to offer. And when that fear of desolation reached its peak, we find Christ crying out, "My Father, if it is possible, let this cup pass me by" (Mt 26:39).

For many youths the experience of the human condition is no longer tolerable. Yet, unlike Christ who in praying to have the cup lifted found renewed strength to continue on, these youths surrender to the pain of their life and attempt to remove themselves from the cup of life through suicide.

Helping these adolescents through this darkest of hours is a role not to be taken lightly. Youth ministers may well be asked to "remain and stay awake" for more than an hour, and it is a responsibility for which it is important to be prepared.

Adolescence: An Especially Susceptible Period

The headlines are all too often filled with reported attempts, some successful, of adolescent suicide. The question often resounds: "Why should one entering the prime of life be so foolish?"

Hopefully, the preceding chapters have helped to increase an appreciation of the point that entering this stage of life is often an excruciatingly painful experience. Susceptible to depression, failing to find support from the significant others in their environment, and feeling hopeless and helpless, adolescents are often left with a sense of total despair. When all other resources appear to have been exhausted and insufficient, escape may be seen as the only viable option for problem resolution. When the problem is "life," then escape is death!

Consider the story of Robert; it is a tale all too frequently replayed throughout the "community" of youth.

"Well the early years were O.K.—you know, I was good in school, kept my room neat . . . and all was right with the world. Ha!

"Starting in high school things started to change. I found that I didn't seem to fit in anymore. I was out of step with everybody—my friends, my family . . . the world!

"Throughout high school I pulled back. I didn't have anything to do with anybody. The crazy thing is that it didn't seem to bother me. In fact it was kind of a "pleasant," numbing existence. What the hell—it was that or continue being humiliated and hurt by people who would turn their backs on me and stab me in the back anytime they could. Nobody gives a damm except for themselves—you know, be out for number 1.

"By the end of my sophomore year I started to hate myself . . . to hate waking up . . . to hate life. I can remember telling my parents how I couldn't stand it anymore and it would be better if I died. Damm it! Even they turned their backs. You know what they said—it's just a phase. Phase! Hell, it was my life . . . and it was horrible.

"I felt like a fool. Why did I open my mouth? Nobody really understands . . . nobody really cares.

"It was just a little while after this that I tried to kill myself for the first time. I took a bottle of aspirin and was lying on my bed. I started to get nausea and began to throw up. My dad came in and yelled at me for making the rug a mess. Talk about absurd! Here I am trying to kill myself and he's worried about his damm carpet. I yelled at him: 'I

don't care about your carpet. I'm trying to kill myself.' His
response was: 'Next time don't be so sloppy about it!'
     "I couldn't believe it. Everything I did was either cute
or simply stupid. Nobody took me seriously. In fact I tried
six more times and it got so bad that even the emergency
room people were saying things like, 'Oh it's you again.'
     "It was clear that the only way I was ever going to be
taken seriously was when I was dead. I swear I was going
to do it right this time. I guess I should be glad you and I
met, but I'm not sure if it's any use."

Robert's story while reflecting his uniqueness shows the anguish, the isolation and the general sense of hopelessness exhibited
by most adolescents contemplating suicide. His story also demonstrates the "ambivalence" felt by the adolescent contemplating suicide. They wish to live . . . but without pain. They wish to live . . .
but they need to be heard. The statistics, however, suggest that all
too often they are not taken seriously, not heard.
     Over the last twenty-five years, suicide among the young has
risen nearly two hundred percent and is the second major cause of
death among persons of ten to twenty-five. Statistics about suicide
for adolescents vary and are hard to validate. Reports have estimated
that 400,000 from fifteen to twenty-four attempt to commit suicide
and over 4,000 actually succeed.
     But the statistics, while highlighting the extensiveness of the
problem, do little to reflect the intensity of the pain and desperation
exhibited in the act. Many young people who commit suicide never
had one other person they could trust and admire. Psychiatrists, psychologists and other mental health professionals are rarely the first
to detect a potential suicide, nor are they generally sought out by
troubled youth as "potential significant others" in their life. Those in
the first line of contact are more likely to be family members, family
physicians, teachers, close friends and youth ministers. Each of us is
a potential point of contact.
     Ambivalence is always present in the potential suicidal—the
wish to live and the wish to die are simultaneously present. Those
who are familiar with the clues, the warning signals of an adolescent

contemplating suicide may well be able to snare that ambivalence and use it to save a young life.

Predisposing Conditions

A number of factors or conditions have been found to be associated with the high risk of suicide. Persons in youth ministry, with these special concerns for life, need to become more aware of the existence of these conditions especially as they come to bear on the suicidal potential of any one youth with whom they may be working.

Depression

While every person suffering from a depressive disorder does not attempt suicide, depression is always a cause for serious concern. The sense of loneliness, hopelessness and helplessness which accompanies depression often blocks the adolescents' ability to define and resolve the real problems facing them. Often these youths conclude that the problems are simply unsolvable. Through the distorted prism of depression, there is an inability to see the total spectrum of options open to them. Thus they often conclude that the only two options available to them are either to continue this "unbearable" existence or to escape through death.

Victimization

Frequently youths contemplating suicide will report feeling misunderstood, unfairly punished or alienated.

Many high risk youths feel victimized by their destinies and family histories. Many report family histories of psychiatric problems, especially alcohol and/or substance abuse, and a history of suicide attempts by other members of the family.

Loss

The real or imagined loss of a loved one or the loss of an educational, social or economic opportunity may serve as a catalyst for suicidal action. A history of significant loss, particularly loss of a parent, has been associated with suicide attempts. Research, for example, has found that the rates of parental absence and parental unemployment were found to be significantly higher for suicide attempters. Emotional loss and detachment are often reported in those circumstances wherein the parent is physically present to the youth. Often the youth attempting suicide experiences parental indifference or even an active wish to be rid of the child.

In addition to the loss of parental support, suicide attempters often are shown to have failed in their efforts to establish or maintain significant peer relationships outside the home. They find themselves socially and emotionally without support. Being cut off from their parents, and socially isolated from peers, with no close friends, the youths feel totally abandoned and doomed to continue their pained existence in isolation.

Increasing Pressure

Quite often youths contemplating suicide feel overwhelmed by the environmental pressures with which they are forced to cope. Family problems, failure to make good grades or to be accepted into a group, an argument with a friend—such factors are often magnified to a point of being unbearable and thus act as stimulants to suicidal considerations. Quite often it is a conflict with parents or another significant person in the youth's life which acts as the primary precipitating event to an attempt at suicide.

Increasing Emotional Instability

For some youths, suicide is not an attempt to escape pain or hopelessness but is the result of their total personal-psychological disintegration. In such a case, suicide represents a desperate response to the total disintegration of ego function. The youths experiencing a psychotic break or a drug/alcohol induced hallucination may report that they were "instructed" by "voices" to "go and kill yourself."

The Role of Youth Minister

When confronted with a person talking about suicide, most people wish they would go away. It is overwhelming to be faced by youths who may be thinking about taking their own life. Questions such as "What am I to do? Can I cause them to go over the edge? What should I say" speed through the minds of anyone in youth ministry facing such a situation. While there are many potential *do's* and *don'ts*, the first do is a don't: Don't panic, and don't run away from the youth needing support.

Recognizing the Potential Suicide

In addition to demonstrating care and understanding of the seriousness of the youth's situation, there is a need to know how to intervene in a way which helps not only to diffuse the immediate crisis but also to assist the youth in engaging in ongoing professional assistance.

Perhaps the most helpful thing a youth minister can do is to provide early identification of high risk youths and assist parents to recognize and intervene with these troubled youths. Early detection of suicide potential requires a knowledge of the predisposing factors and precipitating causes as well as an openness to subtle communication of thought and feeling.

The Cry for Help. The surest, most obvious, and yet often the most ignored warning signal is the suicide attempt itself. Statistics suggest that two-thirds of those who committed suicide had attempted it earlier.

One of the most dangerous myths is that those who threaten or talk about suicide won't go through with it. Such is not the case, and as a youth minister one *must* take seriously all such suggestions by adolescents that they maybe contemplating suicide. One may be in the position to hear their last cry for help—and their cries cannot be taken lightly. Comments such as "Everybody would be better off without me," "I just want to end it all," "What's the use?" and "I can't take it anymore" all need to be taken seriously.

Quite often the suicide attempt expresses a call for a response from the significant others in the environment. It is a call for attention, for affirmation, and a sign of caring. It is not always a reflection of a desire to die. In such an instance one should not be afraid to ask youths making such threats or comments if they are really thinking about committing suicide. The mention of suicide will not plant the idea. Rather, it will relieve them to know that they are being taken seriously, and that they are better understood than they may have suspected.

The youth considering suicide often hopes to use a suicidal attempt as a means of eliciting love, care, and affection, yet many times it just does not work that way. As was the example with Robert, quite often the parent responds either with total disinterest or with anger at the inconvenience brought into their life because of this "stupid," "silly" kid. Failure to provide the needed affirmation and caring response only serves to highlight their loneliness and hopelessness and moves them to consider suicide not just as a call for help, but as a potential solution to their pain.

Investing in Death.   Often the indications are less direct. For example youths may attempt to secure the means of suicide such as sleeping pills, a gun, or a rope. These actions must be taken very seriously. The response that they "are doing this just for attention" may be valid, but it is attention that you must supply or else they may escalate their attempt for attention to the point of taking their life. As noted in the introductory comments of this chapter, even Christ in his darkest moments needed to call out for support. So, too, are these youths in crisis calling out for support, and one should not dismiss the reality that one's presence to these adolescents may be God's response to their call.

Other youths may be even more subtle in their attempts at conveying their feelings or concerns about death and suicide. For example adolescents may begin to discuss the legal disposal of personal property. They may question about the handling of documents or wills and talk about another person's suicidal thoughts. Others may inquire extensively about death and the hereafter.

While each of the above topics of inquiry may represent simple curiosity, they also might reflect attempts to get "their house in order" prior to committing the act. Signs such as these need to be seen as potential invitations for help.

Withdrawal from Life.   Not all youths are as specific in their expression of their suicidal concerns or interest. Often, it is the "withdrawal" from life rather than the active interest in death which signals a potential for suicide. Rather than providing direct verbal warnings, many youths use their actions as warning flags. Often these adolescents show abrupt changes in their behavior. The youth who has suddenly pulled back and cannot talk to his or her parents, or who is withdrawing from social engagement, or who is exhibiting difficulty sleeping or eating, may be providing signals of a vulnerability to suicide. The youth at risk may exhibit markedly increased anxiety and tension, with a rapid and sharp decline in efficiency and school performance.

As youths pull further away from life into despair, they may begin to dispose of prized and valued possessions—a radio, TV, camera or sports equipment. Often such giving away represents an attempt to disassociate from the last of the reasons or reflections of life.

While there are many potential predisposing factors and signals for a youth at risk, those most frequently associated with suicide can be found in Table 9-1. It would serve everyone well to become more familiar with these signals or cues so as to be better prepared to recognize and respond to the youth's invitation to "stay for one hour."

What To Do—Where To Turn

A youth contemplating suicide is a youth in both immediate and long term crisis. The nature of the crisis is such that it requires a two-pronged approach to intervention. Phase 1, Crisis Intervention, is the one in which the youth minister may find his or her particular place as helper. The second phase of treatment requires a more ongoing, in-depth, professional therapeutic relationship. Yet even during this second phase the youth minister may serve a supportive role.

Phase 1: Crisis Intervention

Treatment for adolescents attempting or considering suicide often takes a "life line approach." What is essential is that the youth minister form a therapeutic alliance with these adolescents. This alliance can signal to the youths that in the helper's estimation they

Table 9-1:
Checklist of Early Warning Cues

- any sudden change in usual behavior
- withdrawal from family and friends
- giving away cherished possessions
- severe changes in eating habits
- preoccupation with physical symptoms
- visits to family physician with trivial complaints
- neglect (as a change) of personal appearance
- changes in personality (sullen, aggressive, defiant)
- change in the type of friends
- use of drugs and/or alcohol
- sexual promiscuity
- changes in mood with withdrawal, loneliness and isolation
- preoccupation with death in thoughts, drawings, scribbles, letters
- signs of depression
- loss (death in family)
- dissolution of social relationships
- signs of self-deprecation as inadequate
- expressed feelings of helplessness and hopelessness
- expressed feelings of loneliness, isolation and alienation
- increased impulsivity
- recent experience with suicide of another

and their life are of the utmost importance and that there is a willingness to do anything and everything to preserve it.

Working with suicidal youths requires that one remain available. Their need for emotional support may not coincide with one's scheduled appointments; thus there is a need to remain flexible. Once contact is made it becomes essential that the youth minister tune in, understand, and intervene.

Tuning In. As noted previously a suicidal threat or statement by an adolescent should never be taken lightly, laughed at, or dismissed as preposterous. It is essential that one tune in to the youth's concern and attempt to diffuse the immediate situation by allowing ventilation about the various concerns and frustrations. Almost nowhere else in the helping process is listening so essential. This is not a time for a pep talk, empty phrases, or lecturettes, especially any on the "sinfulness" of suicide. There is a need to be warm, accepting and totally attentive; this conveys to the youth that the threats and complaints are being taken seriously.

Conveying Understanding. In addition to allowing an opportunity for ventilation it is also important to begin to understand the issues underlying the crisis. In listening and reflecting an understanding of the situation, one must avoid glib reassurances which may communicate a lack of understanding of the real seriousness with which the youth comes to this situation. Expressions such as "It will be O.K." or "It really isn't that bad," or the mistimed directive to "ask God for help" may be misinterpreted as evidence that, like most others, one doesn't see the realness of the youth's desperation.

While there may not be a full understanding of all the issues underlying the youth's pain, one can and must convey an understanding of the existence and intensity of the pain being experienced. The youth needs to feel that the pain which is unique to his or her life condition as well as that which is exacerbated by this adolescent developmental phase is being understood.

In addition to "hearing" the pain being expressed, you must be attentive to and reflect your understanding of the youth's own ambivalence about the suicide. Demonstrating your understanding and acceptance of the strong, painful feelings that led to this point will provide the bonds of alliance needed to begin to intervene. Reflection of the "hope" contained in the youth's own ambivalence will provide the "motive" for continued alliance and intervention.

Providing Information. Once an alliance has begun to be formed and the youth feels that he or she has been heard and understood, the youth minister needs to begin to structure through information dissemination what needs to be done.

During this stage there is a need to begin to discuss resources available for problem(s) solution. The youth needs to understand that for every problem there is more than one solution, at least one other option. The message to be conveyed is that life, not death, is the only real alternative. Just as Paul prayed with the Christian community gathered at Ephesus, "May the God of our Lord Jesus Christ, the Father of glory, grant you a spirit of wisdom and insight to know him clearly" (Eph 1:17), the person in youth ministry needs to be an instrument of insight and clarity to the value of life.

In addition to working on the "problems" facing the youth, one needs to let the adolescent know that others need to be informed (parents, professionals, etc.). The youth at this point will be anxious and needs to be told the specific steps to be taken. At this point it is important to explain that you will stand by the youth's side and continue to be available even though the need exists to find a professional who is better prepared to help with the various real and serious concerns he or she is facing.

Contracting.   Finally, the most essential feature of this phase of intervention is to establish a contract to live. When confronted by the youth in pain who seeks answers as to "why" he or she should live, there is a need to remember that regardless of what appears to be the bottom line is that he or she must live. One musn't debate or argue with the youth about the pros and cons of living, or whether or not he or she should live or die. The position that life—his or her human life—is prized, and as such he or she *must* live, is a point which in the helper's eyes is not debatable.

The "contract" is not a legal document or an extensive proclamation of life. It is simply the youth's word, promise, or statement of intent to "hold on." The youth minister should firmly seek to have the youth commit to a "no-suicide contract" in which the youth gives his or her word not to take his or her life during this period in which one is working to find and provide help.

Phase II: Professional Help

The initial stages of crisis intervention are only tapping the surface of the pain and frustration felt by the adolescent at risk. One is not going to be able to simply talk the suicidal youth out of it permanently. The great depths of depression, anxiety, and alienation which prevail in the troubled youth needs much more than that which the youth minister is able to provide. Therefore professional assistance needs to be sought as soon as possible. The adolescent needs to feel, however, that the person in youth ministry (i.e., teacher, cleric, guidance counselor, religious) will be willing and available to continue to listen to him or her as well, and is there to help with making the initial contacts with a professional.

Long term treatment is usually indicated for the more chronic difficulties that predispose a particular youth to suicidal behavior. Family pathology, such as lack of parental involvement and poor communication, along with individual symptoms like depression, low self-esteem and poor impulse control, all require professional attention.

In order to be of service during this phase of intervention, the youth minister needs to be familiar with the professional resources available within the community. There are hundreds of crisis intervention and suicide prevention centers in the United States. Youth ministers need to familiarize themselves with the numbers, locations and procedures of these centers. Often, these centers will have twenty-four hour "hotlines" and provide back-up professional consultation. If a listing of professionals and programs in one's area is not available, then it is suggested that you compile a list by contacting local police, physicians, hospitals, county or city health agencies and the local mental health and mental retardation centers. All of these sources should be asked to identify their various services and programs which are aimed at meeting the needs of youth in crisis, and to outline the procedures they follow in accepting referrals.

Knowing *when, where* and *how* to turn for professional help is an important ingredient to the youth minister's repertoire of helpful responses.

Concluding Thoughts

Suicide, the ultimate despair, need no longer be a major cause of death. Suicide can be prevented. Much more is becoming known about the conditions increasing the likelihood of suicide, the type of person that may attempt it, and why. Also, those in the helping professions know more about successful intervention with families and individuals in crisis.

As the first recipients of the cry for help, the youth minister must have the ears to hear, the eyes to see, the will to be and to remain with the youth in crisis. As a youth minister, one must remember that the gift of human life is too important not to stay "for even an hour" (Mt 26:40).

To the intensity of the youth's pain there is a need to bring the joy of the light of the resurrection. The support and concern of another as reflected by the availability and presence of the youth minister may provide the illumination that offers the youth the hope found in the paschal mystery: a mystery that shows that life without suffering (glory without the cross) is an illusory hope; a mystery that demonstrates that our human sufferings can become tolerable with the knowledge that Jesus too endured them and showed us how we can grow and mature through them.

Recommended Materials

Babkin, Brenda *Growing Up Dead*. Nashville: Abingdon, 1979.

Bridgins, S.E. *Notes for Another Life*. New York: Alfred A. Knopf, 1981.

Ferris, J. *Amen, Moses Gardenia*. New York: Farrar, Straus & Giroux, 1983.

Griffin, M. and Felsenthal, C. *A Cry for Help*. New York: Doubleday, 1983.

Klagsbrun, F. *Too Young To Die*. New York: Pocket Books, 1981.

McCoy, K. *Coping with Teenage Depression: A Parents' Guide*. New York: New American Library, 1982.

Polly, J. *The Living Alternative Handbook*. Suicide Prevention and Crisis Services, Ithaca, N.Y.

Suicide Prevention Center, Inc., 184 Salem Avenue, Dayton, Ohio 45406. A general resource center for information.

Epilogue

Adolescence: Caterpillars and Butterflies

In life, one must often experience two or three caterpillars if one is to know the butterflies. This was the insightful instruction given by the tiny, fragile rose to her protective prince in Saint-Exupery's classic *The Little Prince.*

While addressing her comments to the prince, the rose most certainly could have just as well been forewarning adolescents and those who minister to them about the experience of growth and development through this period of storm and stress. For just as the prince was warned, adolescents, in the midst of their turmoil and parents under the stress of rearing youth, need to appreciate that it *is* necessary to put up with the turmoil of adolescent development if they are to know the wonders of a youth's emerging identity and his or her recognition of God's special plan.

As described within this text, the road traveled in adolescence is filled with its share of caterpillars. The hours of introspection in search of answers to the questions of "Who am I?" "Why am I?" and "What will I become?" make adolescence a time of uncertainty and doubt, a time of pain and vulnerability. Adolescents are poised to question, challenge and re-evaluate the standards of their childhood—standards which have been held unquestionably as the benchmarks for knowing the "who," "why" and "what" of one's life. These standards must, and do, crumble under the critical eye of the adolescent, but as they crumble, so too does much of the support and comfort they have previously provided. Adolescence is most certainly a period of uncertainty, one filled with pain and doubt, stress and turmoil.

But all is not pain and destruction in the adolescent experience.

143

It is by destroying the old that the stage is set for accepting the new, the personal, the uniquely "mine." Thus, the result of the painful soul-searching and questioning is the adolescents' awakening to the special gifts and talents which are theirs and to the special invitation to "become" the persons God has called them to be. Growing in self-discovery and self-identity, adolescents move away from dependency on parents and parental control and begin to stand beside their parents, taking their own place in the world. New friends, in deeper relationships, now serve as the substructure to the next generation's social order. Changes in adolescent thinking and reasoning provide the basis for their increased reflective thinking, expanded vision of reality and ability to dream the dreams of "what could be."

The Road Continues—From Identity to Intimacy

The process of adolescence has opened youths to their many gifts and talents which help to define their own uniqueness. From the pain of adolescents' identity crisis comes the next of life's many roads. Knowing who one is stimulates a desire to share this self with another. It is through this sharing of self that further clarification and insight of one's identity is obtained. The identification of self is a process which continues throughout life. In the later stages of adolescence, youths begin to "see" self as one which is intricately and intimately tied to others. The road of development continues, with the direction being one of increased intimacy and purposeful relating with all.

Responding to Christ's Call

Through these later stages of adolescent development there is a growing realization that the experiences of life, both painful and joyful, are encounters in which the Lord speaks in a special way to each person. The road yet to be traveled by youths is one which challenges them to identify the special-personal relationship to which God calls.

Just as the process, the experience, the journey, is not complete for adolescents, nor is it for those who minister to them. The emerging young adult will continue to search. It is the role of the youth minister to encourage adolescents, late in their development, to step back from their eager search for careers, for friends, for answers to questions of marital and vocational future, so as to pause and quiet the search and become faithful listeners. Adolescents may need help in learning how to quiet their busy days, their harried searches, in order to be open to the unique "life call" which is theirs. Listening to the movement of God in their lives and positioning themselves for personal response to the movements is the task now confronting these youths. Youth ministers may serve as a valuable resource in teaching youths to listen, to pray, to contemplate Jesus and to prepare themselves to respond to the special invitation Jesus offers.

While the book is now complete, those challenges facing adolescents still remain. Identity formation, the unfolding of the abilities, gifts, talents and place in the world which are uniquely individual, will continue. Further, the uniquely special invitation by Christ will forever challenge youth to work through the caterpillars of life in order to experience the butterflies which God has planned.